CONQUER THE C

David Walther

BRIDGETT WALTHER grew up in Dayton, Ohio, and has written for *Elle* magazine, *Elle Accessories*, *Life & Style*, *Fashion Week Daily*, KLM's in-flight magazine, and *In Magazine*. She has also written promotional copy for various designers, including Movado, Stella McCartney, Dior, and Vera Wang, who recognize the connection between the stars and the celestial jewelry, fragrance, and clothing they create.

Bridgett's client list includes celebrities and so-called average people. She has written, taught, talked on TV and radio, and spoken at numerous forums about the power of astrology.

You can access her by visiting her Web site www.bridgettwalther.com.

Conquer the Cosmos

*Use Astrology to Attract the Man,
Money, and Happiness You Deserve*

Bridgett Walther

A PLUME BOOK

PLUME
Published by the Penguin Group
Penguin Group (USA) Inc., 375 Hudson Street, New York, New York 10014, U.S.A.
• Penguin Group (Canada), 90 Eglinton Avenue East, Suite 700, Toronto, Ontario,
Canada M4P 2Y3 (a division of Pearson Penguin Canada Inc.) • Penguin Books
Ltd., 80 Strand, London WC2R 0RL, England • Penguin Ireland, 25 St. Stephen's
Green, Dublin 2, Ireland (a division of Penguin Books Ltd.) • Penguin Group
(Australia), 250 Camberwell Road, Camberwell, Victoria 3124, Australia (a division
of Pearson Australia Group Pty. Ltd.) • Penguin Books India Pvt. Ltd., 11 Commu-
nity Centre, Panchsheel Park, New Delhi – 110 017, India • Penguin Group (NZ),
67 Apollo Drive, Rosedale, North Shore 0632, New Zealand (a division of Pearson
New Zealand Ltd.) • Penguin Books (South Africa) (Pty.) Ltd., 24 Sturdee Avenue,
Rosebank, Johannesburg 2196, South Africa

Penguin Books Ltd., Registered Offices: 80 Strand, London WC2R 0RL, England

First published by Plume, a member of Penguin Group (USA) Inc.

First Printing, March 2010
10 9 8 7 6 5 4 3 2 1

Copyright © Bridgett Walther, 2010
All rights reserved

Ⓟ REGISTERED TRADEMARK—MARCA REGISTRADA

LIBRARY OF CONGRESS CATALOGING-IN-PUBLICATION DATA

Walther, Bridgett.
   Conquer the cosmos : use astrology to attract the man, money, and happiness you
deserve / Bridgett Walther.
      p.   cm.
   ISBN 978-0-452-29585-8 (pbk. : alk. paper)   1. Success—Miscellanea.
2. Astrology.   3. Zodiac.   I. Title.
   BF1729.S88W35   2010
   133.5—dc22

                                                          2009028582

Printed in the United States of America
Set in Galliard
Designed by Eve L. Kirch

This book is dedicated to my husband, David,
who has stood by me through his many health challenges,
and always provided love, another point of view,
and emotional support.

CONTENTS

FOREWORD

It seems I've always known the word "astrology." Growing up I was surrounded by my parents' friends—beautiful, exciting young people who were all actors, models, singers, and artists. They were always discussing so-and-so's sign, saying things like, "Well, it figures if he has a Pisces rising," so I knew the signs of the zodiac before I knew the alphabet.

From the time I was young I've understood the power of astrology, and I believe to this day that astrology can be a great tool in providing insight into human nature. It unravels the mysteries of our wonderful and complicated fellow human beings and helps us understand why we do the things we do to ourselves and to each other.

I've known Bridge for longer than I can remember. She is definitely the real deal. I've called her at the crack of dawn to talk about boyfriends, children, houses, careers, you name it. I always ask for her advice.

Have fun with everything you will learn from Bridgett!

—Cher (Taurus with Cancer rising)

ACKNOWLEDGMENTS

Thanks and endless love to my husband, David, who knew I had a book in me and put up with my moods, and to my kids, Ethan, Trudy, Seth, Shilpa, JT, Julianne Rose, and Andrew Raj, who constantly cheered me on. Special thanks to my sister, Mary Trueschel, for believing in me. Also much love and gratitude to Cher for offering to write my foreword and encouraging me to write this book. Thanks to my literary agent, Meredith Dawson, for promoting my work and watching my back with Virgo precision. Thanks to Becky Cole, my tireless Scorpio editor at Plume/Penguin. A hearty thanks to my remarkable, loving, encouraging friends: Nancy Oliver (who knew this would happen), Bonnie and Steve Hutton, Terrence McKee, Stephanie Heaton, Richie Sambora, Pip Farquherson, Hazel Dixon-Cooper, Holly Gleason, Margery Leedy, Jodi and Steve Wells, Polly Jackson, Carrie Ann Baade, Holly Millea, E. Jean Carroll, Signe Pike, John and Kathleen Walther, Barb Pakula, Girish Sethna, Shivan Sarna, Fred Haussmann, Michael Keisman, Nicole Williams, and Julie Vadnal. I also wish to thank my devoted Web site visitors, who are just as excited as I am about birthing this book.

INTRODUCTION

Are chance encounters meant to be—or do you have to help them along by showing up at the right place at the right time? Do certain talents come naturally to you while others seem out of reach? Why does one man make you ache with desire while another man doesn't even merit a second glance? The answers to all of these questions may be twinkling in the stars.

Whether you're a fiery Aries or a formidable Scorpio, your sun sign plays a role in every choice you make—from what career you pursue to who you will marry. Astrology dictates your personality traits, habits, and mental patterns. For over five thousand years, scholars, priests, and wise men have noticed that at certain times of year, when planets align in specific patterns, predictable events occur. These same scholars and wise men documented that people born on certain days, in particular locations, and at specific hours had noticeable qualities and discernible potentials. All over the globe in ancient times, when a royal baby was born a chart was cast for that child who would someday become king or queen. Now, thanks to modern, insightful astrology, we all have the privilege of understanding our potential and our gifts.

This book explores your secrets, divine gifts, powers to seduce and persuade, and, most of all, enormous strength and potential. You'll also learn how to use your cosmic assets to enjoy a more vibrant, fulfilling life—now and in the future. You'll learn more about the unique differences in your makeup that affect your relationships with your friends, your family, and your potential romantic partners. Once you harness the power of the stars, you'll be amazed at what you can do.

How I Came to Believe in the Power of the Planets

I don't recommend the path that led me to understand and appreciate the power of astrology. Many years ago, I was in a horrible car accident on a two-lane bridge. It was a head-on collision with an oil truck. The paramedics who arrived on the scene thought none of us involved stood a chance, but somehow I lived. I had to learn to walk again after many surgeries and an extended stay in the hospital. During this life-changing experience, I left my body many times. The first time was right after I was transported to the emergency room. I stopped breathing, had no pulse—and suddenly no longer felt any pain. In fact, I felt more comfortable, cozy, protected, and better than I'd ever felt. I

loved the ease, peace, and pleasing, loving place I was entering. There was no pain, worry, or fear. At age nineteen, I
got to experience Paradise, and it was so incredibly inviting.
Suddenly, though, I thought of my parents and became
scared for them. I thought, "I can't leave them—not yet."
Immediately, I felt pain in my chest, head, and back and
heard someone say, "We've got a pressure: thirty over"—
and I couldn't hear the rest. I was back, but I couldn't see
because my eyes were swollen shut. I tried to talk, but there
were tubes in my mouth, and I still couldn't feel my legs. I
wondered about the others in the car. No one talked about
them.

The experience changed the direction of my life. Suddenly I recognized that no one is guaranteed anything. It
was a miracle that I survived, learned to walk again, and
actually became a competitive athlete despite my injuries.
And later I had beautiful, healthy children, the heart and
soul of my being.

A couple years after my accident, I was introduced to a
well-respected astrologer, who drew up my chart. She men-
tioned the day (and time of day) that my accident occurred.
She finished our session saying, "You died that day." She
described the impact of transiting Pluto conjoining Mars
and Saturn in my ninth house and then added, "And you
were reborn."

From that day forward, I began to obsessively study
astrology. I read, took lessons, and learned the fine art of
calculating a chart without a computer. I cast charts for
friends and family members. I asked them what happened

on particular days that stood out as life changing and received answers such as "My aunt died," "I got engaged," and "I found out I was pregnant." I was hooked and there was no turning back.

In this book, I will share what I've learned after years of studying, casting charts, teaching, interviewing, and speaking to groups about the uses of astrology. I've watched astrology grow exponentially during the years into specialty niches, such as political astrology, financial astrology, and weather astrology. My heart and soul, however, are forever entwined with personal astrology—astrology that explains why we attract certain people, patterns, and events into our lives.

What Astrology Can Do for You

From the moment we are born, we're on the clock. Our birth time and location determine our rising sign and the precise degree and placement of each celestial body. Our birth chart is the baseline we use to understand basic character traits, family circumstances, built-in gifts and fears, health issues, and so much more.

Because the sky is always moving and planets have regular, predictable patterns that change at specific times, we can predict the future for an individual or even a country. By comparing our baseline (natal) chart with ongoing changing planetary patterns, we can prepare ourselves for upcoming romantic liaisons, job changes, travel or moving plans, and health or wellness challenges.

Astrology informs us of patterns that have always been with us. These are planetary patterns that we cannot change—but can prepare for and adapt to. The planets are powerful, but you can alter the course of your life to find harmony if you know how to work in conjunction with the universe. Most people say they want to change, but we often revert to old habits when things get stressful or, conversely, when comfort leads to complacency.

I don't like to be surprised by something I could have prevented simply by using astrological timing. So my mission is to share what I've learned from years of study and experience about the endless benefits of astrology. None of us can be absolutely bulletproof, but I'd rather take my chances on planet earth with a reliable assist from astrology.

How to Use This Book

I want you to use this book to help yourself and those you love. I want you to give yourself permission to break free of patterns that have held you hostage and to work with your strengths to become the happiest, best woman you can be.

Each of the twelve chapters begins with a detailed description of one sign's personality; it describes why, if it's your sign, you repeat behaviors that have yet to make you happy. You'll find advice on how to change these behaviors. I discuss the details that create noticeably unique personality traits within each sign: the *decanates* (the three ten-day sections of each sign that reveal surprising characteristics you possess). I show you how to determine which decanate influences you and how to use it to understand yourself and others. I also mention what *element* your sign is: Fire, Air, Earth, or Water—an indicator of your energy and life force. Finally, your action and thinking style is reflected in your sign's *quality*: cardinal, fixed, or mutable. Each detail gives more information about your sun sign.

Your character analysis is followed by a list of celebrities who share that sign, and then a section matching your sign with a member of the animal kingdom, a career and money section, a health section, and a friends and family section.

Then we look at love. I'll help to explain why a feeling of attraction is so strong and whether you should trust that instinct and pursue a lifelong bond or whether you'd be better off channeling that energy into a nice, healthy run— in the opposite direction.

You'll discover that there are ways to smoothly work through what are commonly thought of as built-in relationship difficulties. You'll learn that some of the so-called bad combos are often the most durable and desirable if you've got the guts to stay the course. I've included a sign-by-sign compatibility guide that might surprise you because it deals with real-world relationships instead of fairy tales that rarely pan out.

You will also get some useful advance notice at the end of each chapter about what your future holds—valuable preparation to get your next several years off to a strong start.

Each chapter ends with smart tips to help all of us avoid

faux pas when interacting with this sign: edicts such as "Never bad-mouth a Cancer's mom."

You will also notice that I give dates for the beginning and end of each sign. Keep in mind that the earth's wobble will change these dates from year to year. The stated dates in each chapter are an approximation of the sun sign's transit. For example, in 2009 the sun entered Aquarius on January 19, whereas in 2008 it entered Aquarius on January 20. For those of you eager to do a little research, you can Google an online ephemeris (a table of the changing locations of celestial objects) that not only helps you pinpoint exactly when the sun changes signs, but also when the moon and all the planets change signs. Most ephemerides also include asteroid transits. You can get as complicated and thorough as you want.

Astrology has come a long way during the past five thousand years. Many of my clients and site visitors use it to make smart business and financial decisions. Countless clients use it to time the exact day and hour to schedule their wedding, get on a plane, conceive a child, or buy or sell a house, stocks, or their newest clothing or accessory line. Use this book as a guide—and remember how unique, powerful, adaptable, and rich in spirituality you are. It's time for you to Conquer the Cosmos, too!

Conquer the Cosmos

Aries

You, You, You

Fiery and full of life, you are like the springtime: full of new beginnings, new hope, and warmth. You're indomitable, and you're sometimes given to rages and rants. Your standards are incredibly high, and you don't understand when it seems as though others barely give a damn.

Everything you do involves a certain amount of risk, a boatload of hope, and a powerful belief that yes, you *can* manage this, thank you very much. Few people possess your fire and determination to overcome the odds. You're driven by a higher power: belief in yourself and your cause. You're David fatally wounding the impossible enemy, Goliath. In other words, you are one formidable woman!

You don't necessarily work well with others. You try, you really do, but most people seem so, well, thick. You know what the goal is and have carefully measured the distance to the goal line. Once you step onto the field, you're off like a shot, daring others to catch you or outrun you.

Sure, you've got plenty of physical strength, but the true source of your energy and drive is woven into your mind and spirit. No one can touch your drive.

Famously impatient, you'd rather do most things yourself and, most importantly, your way. Others hem and haw about where to put the napkins and which tablecloth to use. Don't they know that you've already planned the entire meal down to the last mint leaf?

It's not easy being a female Aries. You're all woman, but you just happen to do things as well as or better than most men. Your confidence paradoxically turns on guys and also challenges them to tame you. *As if!*

Your specialty is propulsion. You know how to get parties and excitement started. You start off hotter than a firecracker, but eventually lose interest when progress is slow and incremental. You generally shine the brightest at the beginning of any endeavor. Your greatest challenge is to hang in there and finish what you've started.

Some people find your honesty and aggression refreshing. Just as many are put off and slightly stunned. Whatever. They can learn to cope or get off the boat.

You're the first and most authentic Fire sign. If you were born during the first ten days of Aries, you are the stereotypical Fire warrior: kill now, ask questions later. If you were born during the next ten days, you fall into the Leo decanate of Aries, adding a flair for glamour, style, and brilliant screeching catfights. The final ten days of Aries place you in the Sagittarius decanate of Aries, making you a rolling stone and freedom lover. You're a bit of an intellectual and generally win any argument you engage in. Not only are you better prepared, but you also refuse to debate a truly stupid, angry person.

Besides being a Fire sign, you're also one of the cardinals—Aries, Cancer, Libra, Capricorn—signs that prefer action instead of endless blathering. Of all the cardinal signs, yours is the most action oriented. Fire signs live forever, barring accidents, and you might finally slow down a little in your eighties or nineties.

Stars with your star sign: Reese Witherspoon, Keira Knightley, Victoria Beckham, Sarah Jessica Parker, Jennifer Garner, Mariah Carey, Ashley Judd, Kate Hudson, Aretha Franklin, and Emma Thompson.

If You Were an Animal . . .

Naturally, you've got the determination and territorial courage associated with rams, but the lead dog in a team of brave, adventurous huskies fits you the best. As long as you're strong and confident, you're unbeatable—even under brutal conditions.

Career and Money

Once you're in the kill zone, you really don't care who hears or whose feelings get hurt. You're determined to right wrongs and get justice. You'd make one hell of a D.A., as well as a killer talent manager. Any management job with lots of decision-making freedom will do quite nicely, and you excel in leadership roles of all stripes that require good judgment, rapid response, high energy, and long hours. One category that generally doesn't work well for you is a large, top-heavy bureaucratic organization with tons of repetitive, pointless meetings and redundant, silly rules. You just want to win the award, account, or best numbers and get things done as simply and efficiently as possible.

You need to run the show and probably feel more in control if you own your own business. If you have a big, juicy title at a hotshot major firm or corporation but still have to answer to stockholders and other pooh-bahs, you're not so happy. Having to ask permission to move forward with acquisitions, hires, or cutbacks seems so counter-productive. You hate to have your judgment questioned or nitpicked and can't bear the thought of losing an opportunity because everything must run through the strainer of middle management.

You're a get in, hit it, and get out kind of girl. Sucking up to ancient fuddy-duddies and idiots who are trapped in the past or have a very limited view of the world is insulting. Big corporations may lure you to work for them by offering impressive money, club memberships, power, and prestige, but imagine your disappointment when you recognize that it's all just about playing by someone else's rules.

Starting your own business takes effort (no problem), resources (no problem—you always find a way), and time (could be a problem). You don't like tasks that drag on endlessly. If a business is challenging and exciting enough to keep you passionate through its long evolution, you'll tolerate that beautifully. If it's a job that bores you, you'll move on.

Because of your high standards and intolerance of others' time-wasting drama and pettiness, you're happier calling the shots. This might create some power struggles with people who find you haughty, bossy, or confrontational, and might eventually force you into shutting down your business or reaching a distasteful compromise. You are not a girl who agrees to compromise without punching a few noses and blasting some gut-wrenching salvos. You never just fold up your tent and say, "You are right and I am wrong."

You're not afraid to bash heads with others. It's a pattern and expected part of life for you. When you feel yourself ready to explode, try this: Pause and decide if your argument and fierce stand are in your best interests or will benefit others. Most of the time, your point of view is well-taken and honest. There are times, however, when your temper boils over and destroys any hope of mediation or cooperation. At those times, you'd be better served by counting to a thousand before uttering a word. It's highly recommended that you run your own business your way and always keep at least 51 percent of ownership rights and control even if you bring on a partner. Keep in mind that a partnership demands more time, discussion, and sharing. Before entering into a partnership agreement, make sure you're willing to compromise.

Health

You refuse to give up or give in to things like age, wrinkles, sagging muscles, or illness. You push yourself relentlessly, often past severe exhaustion, and may even wind up in the emergency room if you're not careful.

You're driven to work, work out, and live every day like a champion. There are times when you are forced by illness, family issues, or others' damned rules to back off or cut back. Sometimes the decision to stop something you enjoy (generally a competitive activity) feels mentally and emotionally painful and may lead to depression and anxiety, so protect your workout time. If you have to reschedule a dinner to fit in your weekly volleyball game, do it.

The challenge for you when it comes to health and fitness is moderation. You've heard this all your life and probably still don't understand the concept. You can either learn to approach health and fitness from a balanced, moderate position, or allow injury and illness to force your hand. It's your decision, Ram Goddess.

For example, due to your competitive nature, you're more likely to accelerate the intensity of your daily workout and increase the time you put into it. This strategy works well for competitive Olympians, but is less useful for ordinary people. You may end up with tendonitis, ripped hamstrings, a sprained neck, and throbbing headaches—and that's just from the weight-training part of your program. If you diet aggressively, you can add lightheadedness, vacillating blood pressure and blood sugar levels, problems with your period, skin problems, and overall exhaustion and stress.

Well, guess what, Ram—*you don't have to live that way!*

Compete in one area in your life—either work or physical sports/fitness, not both at the same time. Hire a coach or a trainer who can rein in your compulsive, "watch me beat my personal best" side and keep you balanced and healthy.

Sometimes you need to listen to others and try to do things their way, no matter how convinced you are that your way is *the* way.

Friends and Family

You're pretty picky about whom you spend your free time with and you don't view wasting time on the couch with a roomful of relatives and stragglers all that fascinating. You like to keep on schedule. That means that there is a distinct start and stop time for each event. Without some sort of control, you feel that you're on the verge of losing your authority and allowing others to take over in their sloppy, nonsensical way. Can't have that. . . .

Family gatherings at your house are never loosey-goosey events. Like a military officer, whip in hand, you schedule and plan everything. Yes, Aries: You run a tight ship.

You need to build solid connections with people you can trust and respect—and that takes time. You despise hypocrisy and big talk that isn't backed up by real-time action. Be cautious and observant while choosing friends. It's better to have a handful of trustworthy confidants than a ballroom full of air-kissing phonies.

Love

Men are taken with you. You ride a horse fearlessly, understand football, and change a tire, and you aren't the least bit afraid of hard work and competition. Men relate to you, respect you, and do whatever they can to get on your good side. Warning: Be extremely selective. Most men are too weak and inept to deserve your respect and love. You can outdo, outcompete, out-"man" just about any dude on the street. That doesn't make you a tomboy, but it does make you one fierce woman. Guys love that and view you as the "impossible dream." Some may go so far as to arm-wrestle you, assuming that as men, they have better upper body strength. (*Note to men:* Never challenge a Fire sign woman to arm-wrestle, no matter how diminutive she appears. Fire sign women—Aries, Leo, and Sagittarius—are tougher and more relentless than almost anyone else. Aries women, in particular, aim to win and retain the winning position, year after year.) You're looking for a boyfriend who will skip the party tricks and just act like a real man. As an Aries, it's wise to give each suitor a tough going-over. No exceptions. Clear out the weaklings, liars, and whiny weenies right away.

Your high standards may be one of the reasons why spurned lovers call you 1) *crazy* and 2) your personal favorite, a *ballbuster*. Most men cannot cope with being rejected, especially by a female who knows more about football, hockey, and wrestling than they do. It makes their testicles wither.

An alarming number of Aries women end up in abusive relationships. In his view, they defy the man they're with (or out-"man" him) one too many times. The strong competitive qualities that once excited the guy may suddenly seem threatening, bringing out a violent or mentally abusive side that no one wants or deserves. Just bear this in mind when selecting male friends or boyfriends. Make sure you understand his character and give him plenty of time to reveal his true colors during good times and bad, so you can avoid getting stuck with an insecure loser.

Aries + Aries

This pairing is very fraught. You make each other anxious. You each understand, all too well, the little cues that set off each other's worries, defensive behavior, and insecurities. So with this mind-bending power in hand, you start a debate that will crush your relationship before you get out of the gate. Why bother? When the two of you lock horns, all you get is tangled up. No problems ever get resolved during a shouting match. One of you always has to leave, possibly in shame. This is even tough in a business partnership. Steer clear.

The Bottom Line: You're too smart to settle for this. Extremely difficult to sustain, and probably not worth the Sturm und Drang. **Rating: ***

Aries + Taurus

Surprise, surprise: Contrary to conventional wisdom, this baby can purr like a cat. Sure, there will be times when Mr. Taurus may question your judgment or temporarily slow things down, but ultimately this connection can produce lots of love, success, and intimacy, and a certain amount of protection during your brave battles with authority figures. Having a coolheaded Bull in your corner is a very good thing. It keeps you grounded and more tuned into others' probable motives. You need a little more earth and unconditional loyalty in your life, so this pairing has a ton of benefits to offer. FYI: Spending time with male friends might annoy your Bull. Because you fully understand the parameters of the relationship, you might take umbrage at Bull's insinuations that you're doing something sneaky. You've never been able to do sneaky very well. You're up front and out there. Try to look at this as Taurus just looking out for his favorite interest/obsession.

The Bottom Line: Excellent. Grab on and hold tight. You need the Bull for stability, love, and loyalty. He may question your honesty from time to time (ouch!) but will eventually learn to trust you. You'll earn it, of course. Just view it as another amazing challenge! **Rating: *****

Aries + Gemini

You two bond very quickly. You share the same kinds of goals, dreams, and desires. You also have strong opinions about virtually everything from politics to alternative dimensions. You might find yourself falling head over heels for Gemini's mind and adorable looks so fast that you forget to go down your boyfriend checklist. Make sure he's a stabilizing force in your life. He'll definitely bring a certain je ne sais quoi that you've looked for, but haven't found, in other men. Even so, before you no longer have a choice because you're so flat-out in flaming love with him, make sure he's solid when it comes to handling inevitable stresses, downturns, and other challenges. Chances are, you'll train him. He'll obey the rules and standards you establish. In a way, it's almost too easy—which is one of the reasons why you find excuses to bollix things up from time to time. Gotta avoid easy relationships at all costs. You keep things tipped in your favor by continuously raising the bar and watching how high he's willing to jump, *jump*—for you.

The Bottom Line: Ram Goddess—you've got Mr. Gem exactly where you want him. He's almost perfect, although you may find occasional flaws in Gem's appearance, performance, or behavior to judge. You totally *rule* this one. Start issuing orders immediately—chop, chop! **Rating: ******

Aries + Cancer

Who's the boss? That's a serious question. By now, Cancer should recognize that you are and always will be the Boss Diva—and yet he dares to play all-knowing father or authority figure with you. Doesn't he understand that at any moment, his nagging might blow your roof off, like a keg of TNT? This connection is a stretch. You might feel sorry for him and decide to rescue him (repeatedly), but this pairing won't make the cut. If he is an exceptional Cancer man (minus the usual "poor me" rap, addictions, allergies, and all the other Cancerian complaints), you'll view him as a dull, low-paying babysitting job. Frankly, you've got better things to do with your time.

The Bottom Line: Continue moving as far away as possible from this nonstarter. **Rating: ***

Aries + Leo

You two are very hot, gorgeous lovebirds. Nothing and no one can pry you apart. Anticipate at least two kids, some significant residential moves, and a number of career changes. This relationship has it all—lots of fire, a deep passion for each other, a shared belief in miracles, tons of inspiration, growth, and change. You're adventurous and bold, opinionated and sassy. You complement each other's personality. You may from time to time (i.e., daily) compete for control, power, and who gets to tell the joke; but seriously, what's a little competition among very loving, dear friends who make beautiful babies, create a loving home, and generate endless love for one another?

The Bottom Line: Leo is the one for you. Sure he's a flirt (as if you're not), but you need that periodic punch in the ribs to remind you how desirable and irreplaceable Leo is. Still, he has no peer. Snatch him before someone else does. **Rating: *****

Aries + Virgo

What we have here is not a failure to communicate—there is plenty of communication. No, what we have here is a lot of frustrated communication. And anger, resentment, repressed rage, fear of rejection, guilt, and, of course, love. This is not an easy connection. You both feed and nurture each other at times and tell each other off in your free time. Mr. Virgo can be very ironic, which isn't your forte. You just tell it like it is and shrug off the flying spitballs. Mr. Virgo plans out his attack, maybe for weeks or months. He wants to get even for all the pain and suffering you've created. Revenge is guaranteed, mainly because 1) you're a better man than Mr. Metrosexual is and 2) Virgo hates you for making him look like a sad little weenie. If you're looking for a ball or two to kick around, this might be just the pairing for you.

The Bottom Line: Don't indulge in this rotten little mind game. He never forgets a single foul ball. Don't even think about it, unless you're a masochist. **Rating: ****

Aries + Libra

Both of you are cardinal (action-oriented) signs. Libra generally faces facts and passes the remote control to you, in just about every area of life. He may hold dominion in the style and celebrity sector, however, by either working in the beauty, style, or entertainment business or simply having that rarified Libran eye for beauty and glamour. He can help you prepare for a big night out, kind of like a big sister or close girlfriend. Whether this is a relationship of convenience or an actual hetero romance, Mr. Libra knows more about style than you do. Someday, scientists will discover a genetic beauty and style marker, and they'll find it more frequently in Libra, Leo, Virgo, and Pisces than in less fashion-savvy signs. You essentially rule in every other area of life, so this little combo can work out quite nicely as a lifetime friendship, working relationship, or romance.

The Bottom Line: You support and balance each other, with or without sex. This connection can successfully endure on a purely friendship basis. Not especially rewarding in the hot zone but very good in the haute zone. **Rating:** ***

Aries + Scorpio

You're pretty crazy about Scorpio. You don't actually understand how he does it, but he manages to hook you and keep you dangling for hours, days, even years at a time. For starters, you can't understand what he actually means. He talks in a cryptic, sideways manner that contains so many nuances and possible translations that he generally wins arguments or debates. You've tried and failed repeatedly to outsmart him. Relax—you can't do it. Most people are too intimidated by Scorpio to even try. You get big bonus points for actually thinking you have a prayer against such a formidable foe. On odd days when Scorpio isn't feeling well, you might gain a little ground, but you will promptly lose your advantage once he feels better. This is one of the many reasons why Scorpio gets away with just about everything. Your vigorous appetite for sex, sport, and power intrigue him and make him want you even more.

The Bottom Line: Very strange and out of whack, yet oddly durable. This could last a puzzling lifetime. Your friends don't get it—and they don't have to. You and your mystery man have more fun than most people. Hot, bothered, and excellent for acquiring property and money. **Rating: ******

Aries + Sagittarius

You and Sagittarius make very happy adventurous pals and bedfellows. Mr. Sagittarius keeps you in stitches with his accidental gaffes and pratfalls. He doesn't mean to be funny half the time when he's shoving his foot in his mouth, and yet, he's one of the brightest men you've ever known. He's also sweet and naïve one moment and a relentless bad boy the next. You're never bored. He may at times seem vague or disconnected from you. He's probably writing a script in his mind or developing a new biofuel. But, because he's a Sagittarius stallion, he might also be fantasizing about another woman he's got the hots for. You never know what he's up to. That keeps things very exciting and spicy!

The Bottom Line: Really delicious in small bites (affair) or large quantities (lifetime commitment), this one deserves your full attention. Very special and enduring. A total keeper! **Rating: ******

Aries + Capricorn

Here we go again with the "two cardinal signs" dilemma. This could work, especially in an ingénue/Professor Higgins combo or possibly a master/slave fetish blend. No matter how you slice it, this arrangement is going to be a power struggle. One of you is always going to feel like an unappreciated mensch, and the other like a chain-rattling control freak. A self-respecting Aries wouldn't touch this with a ten-foot pole. There is little chance for equality or mutual respect here, no matter how spunky and smart you are. Humiliation may worm its way into this connection and set up a bondage and discipline shop.

The Bottom Line: Are you actually still considering getting involved with a Capricorn? Get over it. Only for those of you who like to be spanked and yelled at does this connection have some appeal. **Rating: ****

Aries + Aquarius

This can work out beautifully. You kind of dig Aquarius and his strange proclivities. His ideas, opinions, and space-cadet personality are totally entertaining. Not only that, but he also amuses your friends, which is very important to you. You don't want others thinking you're missing out—and you certainly aren't. Mr. Aquarius always pops up with something totally extreme. Often, it's so unexpected that others break out in laughter. Your man has the ability to break down inhibitions and social barriers that are pretty pointless, making you very much in demand as a couple.

People lucky enough to spend time with you usually feel better after being in your presence. You have a wonderful, solid friendship, first and foremost, and an enduring mutual passion for each other, as well as shared goals.

The Bottom Line: Together, you generate joy and healing. There's a supernatural feel to this connection. Positive energy and a desire to leave the world a better place are more likely when you two get together. **Rating: *****

Aries + Pisces

This is an alpha-omega blend (you're the alpha, of course), but it can work, particularly if you love being the boss (check), setting the schedge and itinerary (check), and making up the rules as you go along (check). Here's the paradox: As dependent and helpless as Pisces may seem, he's a lot more resourceful, clever, and sneaky than you imagine. You're too confident and ballsy to resort to sneaking around or trickery, but Pisces has honed the fine art of deception to perfection—another reason why Pisces turns out to be a wonderful performer. He's willing to play to your fantasies and be whatever you need him to be. Instead of absorbing all the dirty work yourself, shift some responsibilities toward Pisces, a little at a time. He might deliberately botch it, making sure that he's never asked to make an effort again, or he might amaze you with his dedication, dreamy imagination, and love.

The Bottom Line: This can work but will demand a lot of thought and effort from you. You'll probably end up being the parent and accepting most of the burdens, but you don't have to. **Rating: ***

What Does the Future Hold?

Until 2011, Uranus remains in Pisces, indicating that your day-to-day confidence in the future may be uncertain. The old rules that used to apply and make sense no longer seem appropriate or useful. Your priorities and lifestyle may abruptly shift several more times until 2011, mostly because you'll always be bracing yourself for another unexpected development. Part of the problem is your tendency to overreact. You need to start to practice detachment, for your own peace of mind. And every Aries should carry the Serenity Prayer in her purse. Once 2011 hits, you have about seven years to reinvent yourself yet again. This could offer up some very tasty, freedom-enhancing options.

In 2012, Saturn and Neptune change signs, suggesting that you stop leaving the tasks you find boring, confusing, or distasteful to someone else. It's time to pull in the reins and find out whether or not you can trust certain people. Do your homework. Make sure you're not covering your eyes and ears and allowing yourself to be hoodwinked by a con artist. Be really careful when it comes to financial decisions, investments, and taxes.

How to Interact with an Aries

DO:
- Get out of Aries' way when she is barreling toward a goal.

- Encourage Aries by complimenting her valor, guts, vision, and determination.
- Make life easier for an overcommitted Aries. Even if she fails to show appreciation immediately, it will eventually sink in and be very gratifying for both of you.
- Believe in Aries' ability to overcome adversity and pull off an eleventh-hour miracle.
- Count on Aries for an honest, unvarnished opinion.

DON'T:
- Be late for an important date or event.
- Undermine Aries' seemingly unrealistic dream. Instead, encourage her to pursue it. There are two kinds of people in Aries' world: friends (people who believe in her) and enemies (people who don't).
- Joke about Aries' skills or ability to compete. It's just not funny, especially to Aries.
- Make promises you can't keep or knowingly lie to Aries. She may never forget it.
- Ask for advice or an honest opinion from Aries unless you're prepared to hear the unvarnished truth as Aries sees it.

Taurus

You, You, You

A queen bee, you gradually draw attention away from all the others scrambling for approval. In your soulful, sensual way, you're a standout, even while wearing cutoffs and flip-flops.

From babyhood on, you're a blend of joy, stubbornness, and beauty, all wrapped up in a very touchable package. Most of you have wavy or curly hair, creamy skin, dangerous curves that look great in formal and casual settings, and very strong, capable hands. You are the quintessential Earth sign—actually, earth mother sign—ruled by a time-honored fertility symbol (the bull) and capable of working a long day, nursing a newborn, and keeping a string of boyfriends or husbands happy and panting forever. Most of you get pregnant very easily.

You're superproductive in other ways, too. You can create a new trend with little or no backing, experience, or even a product. This is because you understand what people crave. Forget about wants—you're far more interested in the obsessive-compulsive *crave factor*. You're the original "gotta have it" girl.

Generally speaking, having just one of anything you love is never enough. So you collect friends, favorite accessories, pets, and books that address your special interests.

It's the rare Taurus who doesn't have a few favorite dessert recipes, guaranteed to drive others into sugar swoons. These are usually family recipes, tweaked to Taurus perfection, i.e., with more butter, more chocolate, more liqueur, more crumb topping. More is never enough for you, making you everyone's favorite guilty pleasure.

Sex is a huge motivating factor in your life. You have no embarrassment or silly inhibitions. You view sex as a natural expression of love, desire, and bonding. Although you may have long stretches of time without sex during times of stress, illness, etc., you double or triple up as soon as you feel better again. This continues throughout your life, explaining why you're always better off selecting younger, more vibrant husbands and boyfriends. You know—guys with the chops to keep up with your prodigious sex drive.

But it's not only sex that pushes you like a pack mule. Security, certainty, and acquisitions of specific treasure (money, real estate, jewelry, classic cars, sought-after artworks) are the other driving compulsions in your life.

You could be snotty about your assets, but you almost never are. You seem to take them for granted and don't feel the least bit superior. So even when you're a living doll like Taurus Jessica Alba, people adore you. You generate a lot more love, desire, and admiration than jealousy. The term "earth angel" applies very nicely to you.

Some of the world's best architects, designers, and producers of unique, old-world-quality furniture, art, textiles, and jewelry are part of your sisterhood of traveling Bulls. You put your unique, tasteful, loving touch into everything you do. When you become very famous and megasuccessful like the queen of all Bulls, Cher, you build homes that are so exquisite, stately, and architecturally beautiful that first-time visitors walk in your front door and collapse into a state of ecstasy.

Famous for your unique voice, whether it's smooth, deep, throaty, or operatic, you can win people over with a laugh, a sigh, or simply by belting out a song. Again, think Cher.

If you were born during the first ten days of Taurus, you're the quintessential earthy, robustly sensual Bull. Your appetites for food, pleasure, and treasure are legendary. If you were born during the second ten days of Taurus, you take on many Virgo traits: You're detail conscious, fastidious, privacy loving, and sincere, and you probably have a strong interest in health and finance. If you were born in the final ten days of Taurus, you have some strong Capricorn traits. You make very strong comebacks, are entrepreneurial, and, despite your bold public persona, may be painfully shy.

You are one of the fixed signs: Taurus, Leo, Scorpio, and Aquarius—signs that resist change unless they initiate it themselves. You're solid, strong, and the last person standing after a tornado or hurricane hits your town. People who don't understand you try to tell you what to do—once. Smart people rarely make that same mistake again.

Because you're a fixed Earth sign, you understand the inevitability of change, but may struggle with it. Learning a new skill that someone (an obnoxious boss, a teacher, a spiteful frenemy) is forcing upon you may take longer. This isn't because you're a slow learner. It's because you want to discourage people from trying to force a new task or skill on you ever again. When you're ready and open to change, you'll change—and not until then. Any interaction with you, positive or otherwise, can feel karmic and life changing. This alone gives you major juju in the bedroom and boardroom.

You are very persistent and hardworking when you're put in charge of perfecting changes and improvements that you believe in, like a remodeling job. You never, ever give up.

Stars with your star sign: Cher, Jessica Alba, Penélope Cruz, Renée Zellweger, Uma Thurman, Cate Blanchett, Audrey Hepburn, Madeleine Albright, Barbra Streisand, and Carmen Electra.

If You Were an Animal . . .

You'd still be a bull—powerful, productive, and strong, sporting a diamond-encrusted white gold "Don't Mess with Me" pendant gracing your beautiful neck.

Career and Money

You're a moneymaking machine, once you find your passion. A job is just a tool for paying the rent. Your career should be your *calling*: something you initially resist but ultimately feel compelled to do. Besides your marketing instincts (natural, not learned, and therefore more powerful and savantlike), you don't merely recognize emerging trends, *you create them.*

You put your talents to fantastic use by developing a simple idea for something that everyone will desire (read: need) for themselves, their children, or their friends. You're a marketing maven, with or without any business training, because you zoom right into others' deepest needs, urges, primal instincts, and lust for power, security, and superiority. As soon as you come on board with a struggling business, the sales start climbing. You can create a dreamy marketing campaign that makes a rock found in the outback into a hugely desirable status symbol (with special powers, of course).

You work past exhaustion and may wind up in the hospital after achieving triumph after triumph, mostly because you drive yourself into sickness. On the other hand, you never feel quite complete unless you're immersed emotionally, physically, and spiritually with a person, career, or passion. Once you find your calling, you're unstoppable and are likely to become the best or most recognized person in your field.

Overcoming your natural resistance to change, fear of

failure, stage fright, and other emotional or psychological humbugs is step one on the road to success. Step two is to align yourself with a savvy agent or enthusiastic, aggressive friend who believes that you're the next big thing and just need to *get off the sofa, baby!* You can almost calcify when you're not in the mood to listen, move, or get out of bed. It takes a very persuasive person to push you out of a comfy nest and onto the stage of life.

Once others get a load of your talent, genius, ambition, charisma, and charm, they're hooked forever. You don't just attract friends; you attract *fans*.

You're no rookie in the investment game, either. Sure, you take your lumps just like everyone else, but you also bob back to the surface and intuitively select more winners than losers. Because you're an earthy girl, real estate and land are always dear to your acquisitive, reality-based heart. You like investments that you can see, use, enjoy, touch, and control. Once you hand your money over to a market expert, no matter how reliable, you don't feel very secure about it. Most of the time, you're better off making your own investment choices instead of relying on others.

Health

The parts of your body most vulnerable to stress and illness as well as healing touch and loving contact are your ears, neck, throat, thyroid, shoulders, jaw, teeth, mouth, and tongue. Well, that certainly gives you plenty of talent to work with, but it also makes you susceptible to sore throats, ear infections, sprained neck muscles, dental drama, and, occasionally, thyroid problems. The thyroid problems may contribute to weight gain, changes in your skin and hair, mood shifts, and sleeping disorders, among other things.

During tense times, you may smoke to calm your nerves, to control your appetite, or because you're utterly hooked. Smoking diminishes your gift for distinguishing top, medium, and low notes in fragrances, wines, and other sensual delights, so cut it out.

Your neck gives you away on so many levels. Although you may make an announcement regarding something troubling (an illness or job loss) and articulate it in a calm, soft voice, your neck splotches red, revealing how upset, even devastated, you are. Many of you have discovered how revealing your neck is and cover it up with makeup, higher necklines, or ropes of jewelry. This works for those of you who want to keep private feelings ultraprivate. For those of you ready for intimacy, contact, and closeness, don't hesitate to reveal this vulnerable, emotional part of your body.

As far as your health and longevity are concerned, comfort, security, beauty, and love are the world's best medicine.

Friends and Family

You embrace friends and family with fervor and loyalty. Once someone has won your heart, it's generally for keeps, so there's not a huge difference between friends and family as far as you're concerned. You enjoy the closeness, comfort, and pleasure they offer, no matter where they're from or how they stumbled into your life.

There is no sacrifice you won't make to help a loved one. Over and over again, your loved ones and friends tell you that they couldn't manage without you. So true. Your special brand of love and devotion is unforgettable and generally spoils a friend for anything less.

You're the first one to answer an emergency call for a friend or loved one. It doesn't occur to you to shirk taking care of a wounded pal. You have a very giving temperament, generous in affection and physical warmth. Once you show up, everyone can take a deep exhale and relax. You bring perspective and comfort back into focus simply by showing up. That's real power, Taurus.

When the chips are down and a friend or family member needs help, your name is the first one that comes to mind. You have a way of calming, comforting, and consoling others that makes you, literally, a lifesaver. During hard times, you're the one who keeps things together and also patches others' egos back together. Your physicality alone brings a kind of security and sweetness. You enjoy contact. Others in trouble generally need more loving, attentive contact. No one has a better bedside manner than you, darling, making you constantly in high demand.

You do expect loyalty and some form of acknowledgment for all your hard work and sacrifice. You might allow a friend to get away without thanking you once or twice, but after that, you feel slightly wounded. Yeah, you notice when others don't appreciate your love and yeoman effort, so give those ingrates the old heave-ho.

There may be spats that put temporary distance between you (sometimes for years), but nothing permanent is strong enough to separate you from the people you love the most. You're very forgiving. No wonder others adore you!

Love

It's a must that you surround yourself with friends and family who unconditionally love you. It's also important that you surround yourself with animal friends. You're a person who hungers for contact comfort and the healing power of touch. Being without someone to snuggle with interferes with your ability to heal.

When you choose a mate, you look for a couple of things: 1) his potential to produce healthy offspring while totally satisfying your enormous sexual needs and 2) his potential to attract money and other security-enhancing opportunities. The only time you settle for a Joe Blow is when you're in a bad, mad mood or experiencing some self-esteem crisis. These moments are rare. You, as a rule, are a sexy, successful, man-eating love machine. The rest of us could learn a lot from watching you in action.

Taurus + Aries

Oh, what fun! You're not always quick to get Aries' jokes, but you definitely enjoy his energy. The trouble is his attention span: It's maybe a tenth of yours, at best. That means that just when you're getting warmed up in a massage session or some other prelude to lovemaking, he's done. Sometimes, he's done before you've even gotten started. The other issue for Mr. Quick Draw is his temper. You generally do a slow burn that might go on for days, a week, or even years before exploding, nuke style, all over the perpetrator. Aries is very quick to blow a gasket over the littlest detail—generally something that you hardly notice or have no interest in. You adopt a strong, silent approach to his temperamental ways. You just let him froth at the mouth while your eyes glaze over and your thoughts drift elsewhere. So even though he's got you pegged as a big spender and you're not always sure that he's being truthful, there is still enough good energy between the two of you to at least generate a part-time, friends-with-benefits connection.

The Bottom Line: Keep your options open and let time sort things out. Either he's got the stamina and staying power to be your man—or not. This has possibilities. **Rating: ****

Taurus + Taurus

Aside from ongoing spats concerning privacy, personal property, or who gets to sit in the choice, cushy chair, this pairing can be nirvana. *Pourquoi?* You both enjoy fine wine, expertly prepared foods with an array of rich, pungent sauces, and ambiance that makes you feel embraced in luxury, competence, and love. You adore excess and would much rather have too much of something you savor or treasure than not enough. You both are a couple of world-class hoarders and collectors, capable of overstuffing any home or office, no matter how large the square footage. Because you enjoy dinner parties, you may need more than one refrigerator as well as a large, stand-alone freezer. Space and roominess don't intimidate you at all. In fact, you can't wait to hire a designer and start decorating (some might say *over*decorating) right away. You two lovebirds tend to accumulate so much stuff that breaking up is extra hard and expensive to do. There's too many good times and too much to lose to let go. You stay rich and hot for a lifetime.

The Bottom Line: The term "soul mate" comes to mind. You and your mate travel in style and comfort, treasure friends and family, and grow happy and round as the years roll by. This is truly a first-class alliance from here to eternity. **Rating:** *********

Taurus + Gemini

You believe in taking your time while studying, thinking, eating, listening to music, exercising, and making love. Just as you feel yourself slipping into that hallowed zone of deeper understanding and satisfaction, Gemini changes the subject or the mood and moves onto a hilarious impression of a friend or celebrity (or you) and breaks the spell. You tolerate this nonsense because as annoying as it is, you can't help but adore Mr. Gem. He's cute and great in the sack, and so interesting, alert, funny, and observant. He opens your heart and mind to new adventures you would have never considered without him. He irritates the stuffing out of you when he perpetually (like a biting fly) zips around, breaking your concentration and demanding your immediate attention. Although you occasionally think about kicking his ass, you can't help but appreciate his gift for opening your sometimes-closed mind. You can walk past the same storefront day after day without noticing the name of the business or anything about it. Mr. Gem always notices every peculiarity, every detail, and loads of useless extras. What would you do without this perfect blend of motivation and annoyance?

The Bottom Line: He's very good at loving you and marketing your talent and whatever you're selling. What more do you need? With a little more patience from you and a slightly less frenetic pace from him, this could be a home run. **Rating: ******

Taurus + Cancer

You're the oral gratification twins: fabulous kissers, sippers, and noshers. You take in the world, or at least large portions of it, via your sensuous mouth. Additionally, one or both of you may have nose talent. I'm not just referring to the appearance of your unique nose but also to your gift for detecting delicate low, medium, and top notes in a fragrance. You're fabulous at wine-tasting parties, too. Both of you prefer certain varietals and vintages that you view as the gold standard and compare other wines' subtle or extraordinary difference from what you view as perfection. Aside from a penchant for all things oral, you two really know how to take good care of each other. You worry about one another and remain constantly, almost obsessively, in touch throughout the day. That might be one of the reasons for your cell phone overages. But really, who's counting minutes when love is on the line?

The Bottom Line: You mother Cancer and tolerate his lapses and moodiness better than anyone. He thinks you're the ultimate confidante and sex partner. This traditional pairing could endure hard times and good ones and just get stronger. **Rating: ******

Taurus + Leo

You've got definite possibilities here. For starters, you both adore attention, first-class accommodations, glamour, food, sex, romance, and feeling as if you're the most incredible person in any given room. That's the great news. The moderately concerning news is that you're both fixed signs. That means you each have your way of handling, processing, and accomplishing things. You don't necessarily want pointers from Leo, and Leo doesn't appreciate your well-meaning advice. If you can get past the wounded-ego hurdle (a big one, but you can handle it), this could feel very, very sweet and intensely passionate. You both appreciate the comforts of home and family, and could work hard and create a beautifully landscaped retreat that everyone wants to visit. Your warmly decorated, extra comfy home could become holiday central, the primo gathering spot for birthdays, special events, and parties, indoors or out. You're both family people and may bring children from previous alliances into your relationship—and then have some together.

The Bottom Line: Once you solve the stubborn ego issues, this one can be a megasuccess! There's a lot more to love about this than to complain about. Go for it. **Rating: ******

Taurus + Virgo

You adore Virgo. In fact, you both desperately need each other for motivation; a deep, abiding, loyal friendship; and love potent enough to power an epic romance movie. In effect, you were made for each other—except for a few details. For starters, you're not exactly famous for being on time. Virgo isn't either; but Virgo always comes up with better excuses than you do and gets the sympathy vote. You don't like to be rushed or have your ear talked off, and Virgo (particularly a Virgo under extreme stress or on one of his "missions") tends to rant until your ears burn and your blood pressure skyrockets. There are two ways to look at this: You can categorize him as a Toxic Avenger and be done with it, or you can face facts—he desperately needs you to balance, soothe, and keep him semi-sane. As a couple, you tend to attract lots of attention, admiration, envy, and gossip. You're a bit more relaxed about your appearance and the orderliness of your home or office than he is. Sure, you'll have occasional spats—who doesn't? But this blend could go the distance. By the way, you also collaborate very well in creative and financial ventures. A keeper.

The Bottom Line: You love Virgo, neurotic tendencies and all. You adore him and would literally do anything for him. He might be a moody bitch at times, but he loves you in his own special way. Look, nothing is perfect, but this can come pretty close. Take it and run. **Rating: *****

Taurus + Libra

Chances are, you bumped into Libra at work. Maybe he was married (but unhappy) or separated (allegedly) at the time. *Wham!* An unholy yet passionate office romance begins. It has all the classic characteristics: his alleged divorce or separation; the secrecy and the pure thrill of sneaking around; the gobs of office whispering and gossip about the amount of overtime the two of you put in together. Let's just cut to the chase, shall we? After months, maybe years, of sneaky sex, sobbing phone calls (oh, the drunk-dialing at 3 A.M.!), and promises that are broken with exotic excuses (if he respects you) or repetitive robot reasons (if he thinks you're a dumb sex toy), you begin to suspect that—*gee whiz*—this thang ain't movin' nowhere.

The Bottom Line: He wasn't available the first time you met him and remains unavailable to this day. Try to get this lesson cemented into your brain the first time it happens: No Married, Separated, or Otherwise Unavailable Men—

Ever. The most valuable thing about this is the lesson. *Don't repeat this guaranteed loser experience.* **Rating: ***

Taurus + Scorpio

We have very hot compatibility here—red-light-district stuff, all the way. Scorpio brings a lot of fantasy and power and you bring raw, endless, lusty love. The biggest problem for you as a couple is keeping your hands off of each other in public, not to mention the lengths you're willing to go to conduct your naughty *affaire de coeur.* There's a pretty good probability that one or both of you are involved with someone else, just to juice things up and rev up the sin wagon. Admit it: For all your whining and bitching, you kinda love the intensity and drama built into this compli-cated match. In fact whining, bitching, and drama become a perverse prelude to foreplay and the real deal. You crave one another. Until each of you feels sated with the other one, neither of you can completely let go.

The Bottom Line: Hurts so good . . . and highly recommended, unless you have a heart condition. You bring balance into Scorpio's busy, often frantic world by reminding him that living in the present is *really* living. **Rating: ****

Taurus + Sagittarius

The phrase "addicted to love" comes to mind. This is a powerful, life-changing experience (not necessarily for the best, but it definitely rates high in the obsession/stalking arena). You find Sagittarius and all his bad-boy ways a total turn-on and huge source of, well, overheated, out-of-control sexual inspiration. Do you care that he's already attached? No—not once you focus your eyes on his body, his boyish grin, and, of course, the package that lifts your sexual adventures to a newer, higher level than ever before. Do you feel like a very bad girl? Sure, but the risk and pending heartbreak feel worth it at the time. You're hooked. He's your version of kissable nicotine. There will be moments when you're both sober and alert and calm when you recognize some of the damage your little *liaison dangereuse* could generate, but those moments are rare. One of you (generally him) is always buzzed, making the shocking element of reality and accountability less of an occurrence. In truth, you can bring out the best (creatively) and the worst (socially or morally) during your tenure.

The Bottom Line: Until you fully understand his track record, ability to tell the truth, and financial circumstances, don't give him your credit card or bank access. This ranks high in intensity but low in lifestyle, trust, and comfort. It's your call, Bull. **Rating: ****

Taurus + Capricorn

First, Capricorn thinks you're a goddess and a gift. Second, *what else matters?* You're both Earth babies, full of hard work and security needs, and you love each other to pieces! This one is a lifetime of happiness, shared values, deep trust, and long-lasting respect. If you don't latch onto Cappie and never let him go, get back on your meds or see a shrink, pronto! At times, Capricorn feels almost like a father figure, watching your back, guiding you in the right direction, and providing all the experience he's acquired over his lifetime (he's an old soul, as you know). At other times, the two of you are like wild animals in heat, especially when there's a moment of privacy, with no visiting relatives or other interruptions. This connection is very protective and works miracles for both of you. You can even create a nice little online business together that generates a little extra income. No matter what you two do, you seem to do it better when you're with each other.

The Bottom Line: You belong together. No question, no doubt. This is the astro equivalent of feeling your way to Avalon. **Rating: *******

Taurus + Aquarius

This is just quirky enough that it might work. You're both as stubborn as a chunk of concrete. Settling differences won't be easy because you each need to win and do things according to your particular scheduling eccentricities. At times, you get a minor thrill up your pant leg (after all, it really doesn't take much to get you in the mood) when Aquarius plays Mad Dad Boss. You might prance around like a naughty, sorry little beast, mostly to satisfy his ego needs. This, not surprisingly, leads to foreplay and, most probably, semiangry sex. You'll take whatever you can get and do enjoy the fantasy of being tamed or controlled for brief intervals.

Obviously, it's a total illusion. No one can actually control you or Aquarius. A desire to not cooperate unless forced actually feeds the flames in your naughty incendiary connection. Once you buy property or have kids, it'll be nearly impossible for you to divorce or separate. Neither of you is willing to give up a thing. So, no matter how difficult things might get, this could be a lifelong commitment.

The Bottom Line: This is not for the faint of heart. Go into this knowing that you'll probably end up together, happy, miserable, or something in between. You'll need cojones and courage in equal measure—or just huge quantities of booze and naïveté. Oddly enough, it can actually feel like Paradise to a number of you. **Rating: *****

Taurus + Pisces

You two really click. You bring plenty of reality and earthy sensuality to the table and Pisces offers up imagination, magic, dreams, and flexibility. You don't always agree with Pisces' way of handling things but are swept off your feet by his charm, romantic nature, musicianship, and physical beauty. You gladly accept a pair of rose-colored glasses from Pisces and enter into his slightly surreal world of magic and mayhem. He's not as strong, persistent, or reliable as you, which actually gives you a calling: protecting, helping, assisting, and teaching him the ways of the world. He, meanwhile, shows you another side of life that you've never taken seriously before. So he can be a magic man for many of you.

The Bottom Line: Just make sure he has a real job, no criminal record, and no drug or alcohol problems. Sure, this means setting the bar rather low; but if you want this man-child, you'll have to learn to help him become a man. Might or might not work, but worth a try. **Rating: *****

What Does the Future Hold?

During the next several years, you're in a building, creating, and re-creating phase. If at first you don't succeed, keep trying until you do. View this as a long stretch of spiritual and emotional study. There are no failures—just important life lessons. Some of you might change careers or your major (maybe several times) during this phase. Change and conscious living work hand in glove. Grow, baby, grow!

Another thing: Learn to be self-sufficient. Grow your own veggies and herbs. Make your own soap. Become as financially and emotionally independent as possible during this phase. Bulletproof yourself and your family from financial and political hiccups.

How to Interact with a Taurus

DO:
- Treat all of Taurus's property, friends, and loved ones with respect.
- Listen instead of raising your voice or clamoring for a Taurus's attention.
- Prepare your Bull's favorite meal, and make enough for leftovers. Food makes your Bull feel loved.

- Speaking of love, bless your Taurus with a hug, kiss, back rub, or other physical comfort that feels like love.
- Accept that Taurus lives in her own time zone. If you need your Bull to arrive on time, tell her that the event starts at least forty-five minutes before it actually does.

DON'T:

- Ever push, rush, or crush Taurus's very sensitive feelings. Your Bull might put up with this a few times, but once enough anger accumulates within Taurus, *look out*—and grab your flak jacket and helmet!
- Expect Taurus to pick up the check for every outing, no matter how much money she has.
- Preach about Taurus's gaining a few pounds. Your nagging may actually encourage more rebellious comfort noshing.
- Be cold and unresponsive to your Bull. This is immediate grounds for dismissal or divorce. When your Bull needs love, the *least* you can do is provide it. And if for some reason you're physically unable to offer physical love, start being a lot nicer, kinder, and more forgiving.
- Denigrate your Bull's family members, childhood experiences, or interests. It's not funny and will be interpreted as mean and nasty.

Gemini

MAY 21–JUNE 21

♊

You, You, You

Why would anyone settle for only one personality or exotic accent when you can experiment with scads upon scads of them? Unpredictable, and hilariously inappropriate when you're among trusted peeps, you instantly zip back into Ms. Goody Two-Shoes when a situation warrants restraint.

You're the sexy heartbreaker that no man with decent circulation can take his eyes off: a sparkly star on the top of the Christmas tree one moment, and a forlorn Yorkie left out in the rain the next. It takes some doing (like superpowers, a bawdy sense of humor, a Mensa card, and an injection of industrial-strength sexual prowess) for others to keep up with your ever-evolving moods and shifting attention span. Your eyes dart around while allegedly listening to someone else's stories. Blame your burning curiosity about the fabulous specimen that just sashayed into the restaurant or club. Your mind fast-forwards to what he might look like naked, aroused, and desperate to please you. Then, stage left, you spot a barely speaking couple at a corner table and try to figure out what happened or if this is the final chapter for them. All of these quick hits happen in a split second. Then your eyes move back to the person you're allegedly listening to. You know—your date. Your theory (and you're sticking to it) is that life is shockingly short and *missing out* is the eighth deadly sin. You religiously refuse to miss out on a thing—especially a *man* thing.

Most people don't see or feel the vibrant mental, emotional, and sexual energy you experience in a crowd. You see mysteries in progress, a marriage on the verge of collapse—or a tryst mere milliseconds away from being eagerly, breathlessly consummated. Your extreme imagination can turn each moment into an epic movie that races through your mind. To make your imagination even more interesting, you actually *feel* the sensations in the fantasy you create. That's powerful Gem mojo.

You're the first and most flexible Air sign. If you were born during the first decanate (first ten days) of Gemini you're very quick, clever, and geckolike. You change your mind more often than most and friends struggle to keep up with your warp-speed mind. If you were born during the next ten days, you're more peace, love, and fairness minded. You prefer being in a relationship to being alone. Teamwork isn't a struggle. You have very few problems compromising and adapting. But like the first decanate, you change your mind constantly—only you do it because you're trying to please others. If you were born during the final ten days of

Gemini, you may border on genius, be a humanitarian, and be social when you're in the mood. Most of the time, you do just fine by yourself.

Besides being an intellectually curious Air sign, you're also one of the mutables: Gemini, Virgo, Sagittarius, Pisces—signs that are very sensitive to their environment and tend to be allergic, psychic, and responsive.

Because you're so unique, truly one of a kind, others don't always "get" you—probably because they lack your imagination and astonishing gift for sensing others' emotions and thoughts. This is one of the dozens of reasons why you, Gemini, make a remarkable actress, psychic, spy, detective, or high-end courtesan. You not only understand others' feelings and desires: You share them. You know others better than they know or understand themselves.

Some dismiss you as an opportunist. Sounds a bit harsh, but there is some logic to that description. For starters, you're always looking for hidden benefits or potential pitfalls in business or personal connections. You're on the lookout for successful, highly sexed, smart, confident people. You may look waifish and vulnerable, but you're a tribute to evolution, timing, and superb survival strategy. You may not be the tallest, thinnest, or most beautiful, but you manage to demolish your competition with a whip-smart mind, bawdy sense of humor (when you're on a roll, everyone's face turns scorching red), and profound ability to adapt to change, trends, and a parade of lovers who stick around until you kick them out.

Your self-image may be at odds with the you that friends

and acquaintances think they know. You don't believe in spreading all your cards on the poker table at any given time at only one casino. You like to sample different gaming rooms, see the shows, and compare your physique to those of some of the freakish cosmetic surgery victims you see trolling the gamers with huge money wads. You're a chameleon who scans a roomful of people and sizes up where the freewheeling fun bunch hangs versus where the crusty bad breath bores lurk.

You weren't born to be bored to sobs. You're here to toy with others' minds, jack up the action, maybe invent an appetite suppressant that actually works and keeps you looking no older than twenty-five *forever*.

You're *the* premier trendsetter. Once you get a sense that a look, theory, lifestyle, or exercise routine is on a collision course with cliché status, you're *over* it. You refuse to cooperate and run with the herd. You either lead the herd or leave it. You interpret words and ideas in ways that best serve your immediate needs. You refuse to submit or obey, which is one of the hundred reasons why during childhood you were frequently viewed as an enfant terrible. That wasn't fair, of course. You are an individualist who would rather die than live a life of suffocating ennui. Repression makes you feel sick, which partially explains why so many of you engage in lurid sexual fantasies, and envious acquaintances refer to you as an *enfant gâté*. It's another one of your damn divine rights to think and do whatever you want with whomever you please.

Stars with your star sign: Annette Bening, Angelina Jolie, Anna Kournikova, Jewel, Marilyn Monroe, Molly

Sims, Elizabeth Hurley, Brooke Shields, Helena Bonham Carter, and Gina Gershon.

If You Were an Animal . . .

If you'd chosen to be an animal during this incarnation, there's no doubt you'd be way up on the food chain—a clever, resourceful, sociable capuchin monkey with very sharp fangs and a penchant for biting down hard.

Career and Money

Obviously, you're *perfect* as a secret agent, spy, investigator, detective, courtesan, and actress (even if your main stage is a king-size bed). Yeah, you're the smart, dangerous, bootylicious bikini-clad Bond girl that ties men up, molests them with cruel pleasure, and then makes them leave without their wallet and pants before morning. *Nobody is the boss of you.*

You're great with your hands, quick-witted, and a fast learner. You might study languages and become an interpreter or journalist in a foreign country. You rarely go anywhere without a laptop or smartphone. You stay on top of who's hiring, firing, and expanding. Because you have loyal friends who understand your talent, intelligence, and versatility, you get plenty of assistance when it comes to getting an interview with the top decision maker or a great job.

Saving money is a learned discipline for you. Putting money aside, month after month, year after year, requires a lot of commitment and persistence, which you admire in others but have a hard time with in your own life. You know it's the right thing to do, but you are unlikely to be a smart saver or investor until you find a strong, brilliant financial adviser who can help you make smart money decisions. You need expert guidance in this area and shouldn't plan on managing complex financial activities all by yourself.

Health

Because you look younger than your years (a pain when you're carded at age twenty-five, and a pleasure when you're carded at thirty-five) your vibrant, sexy looks can be deceiving. A lot of you smoke for a multitude of dumb reasons— like the excuse that it keeps your weight down or settles your nerves or gives you something to do with your hands (as if you don't already have five hundred other things to do with your hands). Break your smoking *addiction* (let's be honest about it) and any other bad habits that interfere with breathing.

Addiction can tip your boat, just like anyone else's. While you're trying to "keep your weight down" by smoking, snorting coke, or scarfing down other toxic pharmaceuticals, you're setting yourself up for addiction. You, Gemini, must not head down that dreary road. It limits your freedom. From a vanity point of view, it ages and ruins your teeth and skin. Because freedom and looking young and hot are of primo importance to you, addiction needs to be avoided vigilantly. Even a smart person like you is susceptible.

Keep your air-conditioning system clean and well maintained. Change the filters every month, especially if you live in a hot, humid climate. Your respiratory system, hands, wrists, lower forearms, and ribs all require special care and attention. Nurse Bridgett says: *Too much repetitive wrist movement (eight hours of typing or two hours of hand jobs) aggravates carpal tunnel syndrome.*

Be vigilant about getting flu shots, and avoid coughing, sneezing sickos at work. When you get a respiratory bug, it can hang on for a month, interfering with all the things you love: freedom, sex, high-energy workouts, even talking. Can you imagine losing your voice and not talking for a month? *Horrible!*

Many of you are hypersensitive to fragrance. Certain perfumes may initially appeal to you, but then aggravate allergy symptoms, such as a stuffy nose, watery itchy eyes, and sneezing. But remember that smoking is your number one health enemy.

Your lithe body responds beautifully to exercise that lengthens, tones, and stretches. Most forms of yoga offer that. So do Pilates, swimming, dancing, racewalking, climbing, and hiking. If you're a running aficionado, make sure you stretch before and after each run. You're more inclined to work out longer and more passionately with the right kind of music pumping all around you. (This is another example of how you can "boreproof" an exercise routine: add great music that *constantly* rotates.)

Friends and Family

Others don't recognize how calculating and smart you are because they're flabbergasted by your quirky personality, flirty sexiness, and pitiful crying jags. Drama has been your most consistent gig since birth. You got your siblings into trouble (too bad they weren't as quick and smart as you) by foisting the blame for every wrong you did onto them. It was just a game, for Goddess' sake. So even though you sobbed your dramatic heart out while your sister or brother took countless spankings for you, you impressed yourself with compelling acting skills. Dripping with drama is an entitlement—another damn divine right of Gemini. You're in training from early childhood on, learning all the card tricks that help you get what you want.

Your innocent, eye-batting, giggly personality hides a treasure trove of disparate character traits. Only the smartest, most fortunate, persistent friend will get to see most of you. Showing all your cards and telling everything you know is not a Gemini trait. You're at least as good as (maybe better than) Scorpio when it comes to hiding the truth, shading the facts to suit your purposes, and extracting every last detail from others. Your strategy, which is fabulous, is to spill a few interesting-sounding but unimportant clues in exchange for another's uncensored, top-secret information. Inside every Gem is a spy with a collection of convincing accents and biographies. This talent doesn't only come in handy in espionage; it's also *fabuloso* around party guests, bosses, and moneylenders. Work it, Gem!

You're a quick study and a great actress. You can sit across a table from your best friend's new but deadly dull fiancé and smile sweetly while thinking, *Why is she with this idiot?* You wouldn't dare spoil the mood or forget that the evening is dedicated to oohing and ahhing about your BFF's faux diamond engagement ring while pretending to be thrilled for her. During the entire evening, your strategic brain ponders, *Will their kids be as homely as he is?* You smile and pretend to listen, while writing a play in your mind.

It's fair to say that you're smarter and more imaginative than most of your friends, which is probably why friends and relatives come to you in droves, looking for clues, inspiration, brains, and strategy that no soon-to-be ex sees coming. You're one of the first people to know that a relationship is on the rocks, a friend is pregnant, or a local celebrity is gay. People tell you things. Always have, always will. Protect those secrets like the good friend you are.

Love

One of the things that starts you up is a spicy blend of fiery enthusiasm, dangerously rebellious curiosity (Eve *obviously* was a Gemini), and nausea at the mere thought of being trapped or bored. You dare a man to be a man—to fight for you, take risks for you, and at least *promise* to die for you. If he's great in the sack and brings home big bags of money, you'll want to keep him alive and around for a while. No cabana boy or rude rough-trade dude can trump a really hot, smart, captain-of-industry Big Daddy. Every Gem since Eve has had that all figured out. And, as a card-carrying Gemini, you reserve the right to take a walk on the wild side whenever you please.

You don't need a Mensa membership to figure out that monogamy might be one of the most challenging gigs you ever sign up for. Fact: You bore easily. Living in close proximity with the same person for days, months, or years is bound to settle into a—*shudder*—routine. Hearing the same joke twice is annoying. Hearing it more often turns the man repeating it into a dullard, *at least for you.*

Gemini + Aries

Fortunately, you love variety, rapid results, and especially moody Heathcliff alpha males with enough sexual heat to warm Siberia. On the other hand, you also love variety, period. So Mr. Aries' notorious "I'm gonna tame your ass" possessiveness excites you only once or twice. After a couple displays of testosterone-based anger and jealousy stimulated by his sudden awareness that you had a rich sex life prior to him, you're over it. Your issue, however, is making him go away. Property damage (keyed car, broken window, slashed tires) may occur.

The Bottom Line: Get a restraining order and huge menacing dog, and then get on with your life. Okay for the first couple trysts. After that, it's punishing and unhealthy. **Rating:** *

Gemini + Taurus

There's something irresistible about a Taurus with a big, wide bank account, a palazzo in Italy, and a hundred-foot luxury yacht in Palm Beach. A Bull comes fully equipped, no setup required. This kind of guy is almost too easy to fall in lust with, even if he's married but "almost" separated. You enjoy the lifestyle, sex drive, and power that Mr. Bull oozes every time you bend over or smile. You can run circles around him socially and intellectually, but aren't nearly as adept as Mr. Big when it comes to attracting and growing money. He needs you for fun, sex, entertainment, and a social life. And you need him for fun, sex, entertainment, and maintenance.

The Bottom Line: If he ever gets the divorce (don't hold your breath) this one could be a lifetime of riches, raunchy romps in the bedroom, and luxurious highs and sighs. **Rating:** ****

Gemini + Gemini

You love to get away with things (impulsive flirting, shopping) without anyone busting you and asking questions. You won't get away with much with another Gemini. He knows (or at least suspects) exactly what you're up to. He intuitively knows where you're hiding your latest shopping acquisition—can't fool him—*what a bummer!* And he totally interprets your winks and the meaningful stares that you shoot at your blabbermouth friend; plus, he is uncannily good at reading between the lines. Funny, he's a lot like you. Here's the deal: You can enjoy a long, fabulous, never-boring ride together, but you've got to adhere to certain guidelines. Never embarrass him in public, and do insist that he never hits on any of your friends.

The Bottom Line: This is Spy versus Spy. You both read each other's private thoughts as easily as big-print books. Know when to hush up and when to spill. **Rating: ****

Gemini + Cancer

Charming, sweet, affectionate, and protective, your heart skips a beat around a touchy-feely Cancer. And then you meet his mother and bossy know-it-all sisters. His fam-damn-ily might be a deal breaker, depending on where he positions you on the priority list. It's rare for him to place anyone even a quarter inch above Mummy and Sisties. She gets first place, and first place with honors once she dies. The sisters generally fall into a strong second place. You fight for a healthy third or fourth spot on the family totem pole. Trust and time could change the order of things—but there's no guarantee. Can the sweet, passionate love you share conquer all? That depends on your will, self-confidence, and desire to win.

The Bottom Line: You're all about the present and future and he's stuck in a mommy-dominated past. Get a therapist involved and it might work. Oh—and this connection can attract unexpected money (maybe from Mummy). FYI. **Rating: *****

Gemini + Leo

You're perfectly suited in the romance and mischief department. You love to playfully tweak Leo's sometimes-vulnerable ego. If your Leo is smart enough to play in your league, he parries with a quick jab and refuses to let you get the upper hand. You lap up this kind of foreplay. Always thinking, you audition men by tempting, teasing, and challenging their reaction time, intellect, and sexual potency. Mr. Leo has definitely got what it takes to make things very big, bouncy, and luscious for years to come. You enjoy party games that set the stage for the second act when you're home in bed. He works one end of the room, charming the pants off of others, while you conquer the other side of the room. Plan on a night of sex games and a wild time comparing notes. You're both amazing playahs.

The Bottom Line: Jealousy actually works big sex magic for you two. Watching another woman lust for your man is a huge turn-on. So big and hot that it challenges the laws of physics. *Ka-POW!* **Rating: *******

Gemini + Virgo

Some pairings generate lots of tension along with a deep, abiding comfort zone. Sure it sounds kind of crazy, but this romantic blend can be heavenly and healing or brutally bewildering, depending on each participant's mood swings. This combo requires courage, patience, and tons of commitment (some might call it a test). When it works, it's superb. Both of you are detail obsessed and convinced that your taste is exquisite. You each assume that your recollection of a prior conversation is letter-perfect and correct. Although there will be arguments about shades of differences that don't have much, if any, substance, you understand each other and really want things to work out.

The Bottom Line: You need to have well-defined roles so that you don't step on each other's toes or trounce on each other's territory. You also need lots of stress-busting exercise and antianxiety meds. **Rating: ***

Gemini + Libra

This verges on ultimate nirvana. For starters, you totally *rule* this relationship. Libra is smart—so smart, in fact, that he's actually half as brilliant as you are. That automatically qualifies him for Mensa. You like Libra's style for the most part. You enjoy his desire to please, experiment, and even humiliate himself at the altar of your insatiable lust. Even better, he's willing to role-play during sex games. This automatically gives him more bonus points than the other signs. And because the two of you are intellectually curious Air signs, you can argue every side of any debate without shame or fear of retaliation. You two would've fit in nicely in Marie Antoinette's court. Gossip, celebrity, and excess make you both absolutely *feverish* with lust.

The Bottom Line: This is endlessly fascinating, like a fairy tale with twists, turns, and *sex, sex, sex.* Spoil yourself and gobble this one up. Hallelujah! **Rating: *******

Gemini + Scorpio

This connection has staying power if you're able to make it through the first couple years without getting bored or committing bodily harm. If you enjoy a challenge, it could last indefinitely. For starters, Scorpio keeps you guessing: Is he lying? Sneaking around with his ex? Squandering money at the blackjack table? It's *game on* from the beginning because you never totally trust or believe him. Getting all the facts and details out of him regarding anything personal or financial requires extra help, like wiretapping and accessing all of his passwords. That's hardly a challenge for you. You revel in the excited uncertainty of never feeling sure of your Scorpio. This *not knowing* makes you work even harder to spoil, seduce, and confuse him. *Word to the wise:* Do not work together or put him through school. Start dating him after he's gotten his postgraduate degree and is making oodles of cash. Let some other sap take care of him until he's bankable.

The Bottom Line: Keep your power and mystery in top form. If anyone is going to exit this arrangement, it'll be you, not him. He's smitten and can be dominated and controlled by your devilish sexuality and wit. **Rating: ******

Gemini + Sagittarius

This is a balancing act that generally feels slightly out of kilter. Because you're both whip smart and articulate, you try to outsmart one another. This is fine as long as it doesn't become humiliating or bullying in tone. Because you're both painfully porous to criticism or even a hint of an insult, you both carry grudges, sometimes for a long time. When the two of you decide that a certain ex-friend or ex-colleague is a beast, that person becomes a mental voodoo doll that the two of you blame for everything that goes wrong in your lives. You might also decide that a certain group of people or a business or government entity is the devil incarnate, too. You roast your effigy slowly, turning it over and over, and are able to work out a lot of tension and fear by jointly despising a person, place, or thing. You could spend the rest of your days together, traveling, learning, debating, and criticizing the world at large. Sometimes you'll be the boss, and sometimes you'll permit Sagittarius to think he is the boss. It's an illusion but he enjoys it while it lasts.

The Bottom Line: He's smart, but you're smarter. While he's bookish and creative, you're sociable and sexy. Yeah—he *desperately* needs you to survive in the real world. **Rating:** ****

Gemini + Capricorn

Now we're getting into some steamy yet frustrating turf. You can't figure out what Capricorn wants, needs, or thinks, making him Mr. Mysterious. You enjoy a challenge, but Capricorn tests you in ways that make you question your desirability and feminine power. He abruptly flips from being in heat to withholding sex until he "figures things out." So what the hell does that mean? Some of you get mad and figure that 1) he's gay or bi or 2) he's a big fat liar. But late at night when you're feeling alone, you worry that—*quelle horreur!*—it might be your fault. Here's the short story that encapsulates every Capricorn, male or female: They grow up fast, often without unconditional love, and their emotions are glazed with stainless steel to prevent heartbreak. And yet, when Capricorn feels sexy and hot and pursues you ardently, you feel so loved, sought after, and full-on Jezebel. But for every amazing bit of sexual acrobatics, you also face inevitable ice storms of rejection.

The Bottom Line: The only question that matters is, Do you want this man, with all his baggage, secrets, and emotional war wounds? If you're willing to accompany him to therapy to battle his dark demons, addictions, and propensity to disappear, you might, after years and years, have a keeper. Hmm . . . doesn't sound all that promising, does it? **Rating: ***

Gemini + Aquarius

You're kind of smitten by Aquarius's quirks, humor, odd sense of timing, and extreme intelligence. Aquarius is brilliant in certain fields and way out in front of the competition, but slightly hopeless and helpless in more mundane survival skills. You're a born survivor and have more cures and tricks in your medicine chest than Aquarius ever imagined. So once again, you're a necessary asset in this relationship. You keep Aquarius semitethered to the real world. This could become a full-time job, but one that you might come to love. If you're really lucky, your Aquarius will be hailed as a genius scientist, writer, actor, or humanitarian, and you'll get to enjoy the perks of fame, paid travel, free hotel expenses, and fortune! You also come to adore Aquarius as a friend. You see his strengths as well as his weaknesses. But every little quirk (even the ones with psychiatric labels) seems endearing.

The Bottom Line: This could be a lifelong loving friendship, especially since Aquarius finds you so off-the-charts hot. You feel needed and all your efforts to boost Aquarius in the world pay off exceedingly nicely for both of you. What's not to love? **Rating: *******

Gemini + Pisces

This demands flexibility and a willingness to listen patiently while Pisces finishes his long, wandering, wordy sentences. Since his comments are often filled with confusion, emotion, guilt, and regret (don't forget crying jags), you may feel at times like a proxy for his mom or big sister—a nonjudgmental version of one of them. Paradoxically (your life is bathed in paradox), Pisces may also play father figure or some other protective authority type to your helpless little girl side. There are times when role-playing serves you well. (Anytime you hook up with Pisces, there will be role-playing games galore!) Things get difficult when both of you want to play boss or expert at the same time. Are you willing to hand over the car keys and control to Pisces from time to time? Do you respect him enough to put your fate in his hands? When you first meet, you feel so impressed and enamored. Over time, you wheedle many (if not all) of his secrets from him. Once you see the entire package, it's far from perfect. You now have ammo to fire at him, just in case he steps out of line. This is one of those rare times when you wish you weren't so smart and didn't know so much.

The Bottom Line: One father figure per lifetime is more than enough. Once you see through this man's attractive façade and notice all of his glaring mistakes, weaknesses, and bad decisions, you might decide to return him to his former owner. Oy. **Rating:** *

What Does the Future Hold?

In late October 2009, Saturn moved into Libra, emphasizing all Gemini friendships and romantic connections. Saturn in Libra emphasizes choices surrounding children (have them or not?) and urges you to specialize in *something*. For example, Saturn may influence you to continue your education, specializing in a certain branch of law or medicine or science. Saturn demands results, not just pipe dreams. You may have to choose between two lovers or passions. Saturn forces all of us to use our talents to be self-supporting. Less time is spent wishing and meandering, and more time is spent building a life, business, family, and identity. This phase continues until early October 2012.

The next important Saturn cycle occurs from late December 2014 through late December 2017. During this phase, Saturn falls into your solar seventh house, challenging many of your business and personal relationships. You might weed out a few. This can be a very challenging phase that may result in walking away from one situation and embracing another. Oftentimes, this phase presents as a third party that interrupts a struggling marriage.

How to Interact with a Gemini

DO:

- Be generous with humor, wit, and fast-moving stories with surprise endings.
- Be respectful of Gemini's tightly packed schedge and perpetual time shortage.
- Offer Gemini a healthy snack. Busy brains need food (and love), too.
- Become a reliable source for scientific and financial facts, cutting-edge tech info, and obscure medical knowledge.
- Stay in touch with Gem. If you don't, your Gem will find someone else to talk to. Just don't be a pest.

- Help Gem remain on a healthy diet and exercise program. Be your Gem's buddy in the fight against fat and flab.

DON'T:
- Interrupt one of Gemini's fascinating stories no matter how many times you've heard it.
- Dispute, argue with, or criticize your Gem in public.
- Borrow a book, phone, or treasured gadget from Gem unless you can guarantee that you will return it on time in like-new condition.
- Sneak around behind Gem's back. Your Gem is very psychic and may already suspect that something is going on.
- Do anything that undermines the stability, trust, and unity in your relationship. Secrets must remain so until death.

Cancer

You, You, You

Beneath your strong, capable, "anything you can do, I can do better" Cancer alpha-woman veneer is a trembling child scared to death that somebody somewhere sometime might reject you.

In order to keep that veneer tough enough for any upsets likely to surprise or throw you into an anxiety tailspin, you sometimes add a little fatty padding (or even an extra layer of muscle like the formidable tennis duo, the Williams sisters) to create a buffer zone between you and what feels like a very judgmental world. Some of you become very experienced pharmers, mixing a cocktail of antidepressant, antianxiety, and pain meds to get you through a divorce, breakup, death in the family, move, miscarriage, or depressing betrayal by a once trusted friend. You don't want others to recognize how vulnerable, lonely, and lost you are, so you front a strong, sometimes arrogant visage, designed to keep others at a safe distance. Paradoxically, you desperately want others' attention, love, and approval but are afraid to move forward because of your personal bogeyman, Mr. Rejection. Scratch your surface and there's a beautiful goddess aching for touch, closeness, babies, and home sweet home. But the catch is allowing anyone to get close enough to gently stroke your tough-woman surface.

Like all Water signs (Cancer, Scorpio, Pisces), you were born with a hunger to touch, taste, sniff, and rub up against someone or something you crave. And you certainly have cravings. Maybe it's your mom's famous buttery whipped mashed potatoes or maybe it's that first heartbreaking love that didn't work out. You approach the world cautiously and defensively, desperately trying to control your feelings of desire, need, and hunger. Your feelings are so powerful that they always sneak out, sometimes making you blush (like Cancerian Princess Diana) from joy, embarrassment, and excitement. Darling Crab, your heart is on your sleeve. There's no disguising it.

The phrase spoken by parent to child just before a paddling, "This hurts me more than it hurts you," is classic Cancerian. Every little slight that you think you've initiated eats at your sensitive stomach (you invented acid reflux—congratulations) and tender heart. You feel your way through life, trying hard to pretend that things aren't tearing you up. But they are—and how. If others knew how seriously you take things and how deeply (to the point of physical pain) you care, they might be a lot nicer.

Ruled by the luminous moon, your moods and energy levels are rearranged every couple of hours when the moon moves another degree. It's not just you—or some exotic mental disorder—it's the ebb and flow of the moon's constant changes that determine your attitude. Your moods are affected just like the tides—in and out, high tides and those dreaded lows.

Because of constant ups and downs, raw emotions immediately followed by almost superhuman strength, routines (sometimes duller than dirt) can be comforting. Certain comforts lull your worried, ultrasensitive mind into a less anxious state. You enjoy the comfort of privacy, safety, and a cozy, familiar environment. When friends ask you to join them for dinner, clubbing, or (freakout!) a blind date with one of their friends (double cringe), you do your best to avoid the entire social, dating mess and play it safe by hanging out at home, allegedly catching up on work. Being able to relax and have fun without trying to rescue others or accomplishing something is a learned skill.

Sure, you can be tough, surly, and moody. Sometimes you appear selfish and self-absorbed. But when you're in the mood, you have the most gentle, magical, hypnotic sense of touch. You're a famously great kisser, have beautiful breasts (enhanced or natural—who cares?), and never forget how favorite friends and loved ones take their coffee, tea, or glass of wine. Once a guy falls for you with a thud, that's it: He's a goner. He might still make really stupid offensive mistakes, but he knows that you're a prize catch that he wants/needs to keep—desperately.

As an emotionally wary, yet idealistic Crab, you expect a lot from others. You want them to love you the way you love them. You attend to their every need, and assume that they'll eagerly attend to yours. Not necessarily so. You also expect that your friends, boyfriend, or husband will love your mother—and be smart enough to shut up when you're angry with her.

The first ten days of Cancer belong to the super-Cancer. If you were born then, you're the poster child for Cancerian traits: emotional, caring, sensitive, and attached to home and family. The next ten days of Cancer add Scorpio traits to your personality, making you mysterious, sexual, powerful, and controlling. You feel best when you're in charge. The final ten days of Cancer add a dash of sensitive, music-loving Pisces to your personality. You're more dramatic, have dreams of being in show business, and are extremely creative and psychic.

Besides being an ultrasensitive Water sign, you're also one of the cardinals—Aries, Cancer, Libra, Capricorn—signs that believe in accomplishing goals and are results driven. This adds more practicality and ambition, too.

Stars with your star sign: Carly Simon, Kathy Bates, Liv Tyler, Pamela Anderson, Princess Diana, Lindsay Lohan, Michelle Kwan, Anjelica Huston, Edie Falco, and Gisele Bündchen.

If You Were an Animal . . .

Because of your protective, caring nature, you have the spirit of a mama bear. You shelter and sacrifice for your cubs (closest friends and other loved ones) even if it means forgoing other activities (sometimes sex). Your protectiveness knows no bounds and if taking care of a dear friend or baby means a social blackout, you learn to live with that.

Career and Money

You're stronger than your male Cancer counterpart. You value safety, stability, owning a home, and job security, so steer away from risks. You like paying your bills and prefer being in charge of family financial decisions. Throughout marriages, dating, and babies, you almost always have at least one career going. Your job is a huge part of your identity because it puts food on the table, clothes in the closet, and a decent car in the garage. Responsibility is something you understand a lot better than most of your peers. Sometimes you wonder what it would be like to be taken care of and have no financial worries—just a country club, private jet, love shack in Monaco—yes, please. Then you snap out of it and realize that can't happen. *Why?* Because you will never willingly put your future into another person's hands. You don't trust anyone enough to give up your independence and let him bring in, manage, and spend the money. It's the cost of being the boss, Crab.

Because you're interested in making some real money, you generally have a day job as well as a number of smart investments to fall back on. You and a few friends may organize an investment group or business. You like having your nimble fingers in many pots. That way, if one thing doesn't pan out as well as you'd hoped, you've still got several other pots boiling. As financial planners always say: Diversify. You feel more secure having a solid, safe plan B.

You're not the type of girl to throw away opportunities for stable growth, which brings us to your eccentric band of boyfriends. Why settle for someone who can't hold a job or pass up a chance to get slobbering drunk? Why settle for anyone unworthy of your love, hard work, and deeply caring personality? More on that later. . . .

Health

You always seem rounded and feminine, even when you're rail thin. There's something soft, yielding, and girly about you. Just look at Gisele Bündchen.

You may have problems with your periods, stomach, breast tenderness, and periodic bloating. The first area to bloat will be your stomach, quickly followed by your face. This occurs because of stress, dietary indiscretions, hormonal hell, and abrupt changes in your routines or sleeping habits. *You really need your sleep.* Without it, you're cranky and prone to tears and scary driving.

During moody, emotional times (remember, your moods change as frequently as every two and a half hours), you tend to reach for your favorite comfort foods, such as chips, chocs, tinis, and as much cheese as you can handle without making yourself sick.

So your weight bobbles up and down. Some of you get lipo, implants, butt lifts, or tummy tucks. Some of you try a punishing exercise regime. The happiest among you make peace with your bodies, revel in the beauty of your powerful femininity, and learn to love your so-called flaws.

While you're working on your attitude, you can adopt simple steps like cutting back on salt intake and getting a little more sleep at night. A few quick power naps during the day don't make up for an all-night bender. Physical beauty comes at you fast, but aging comes at you even faster. Make peace with your inner wise woman, your beautiful soul, and your eternal ability to give and accept love.

You need loads of calcium, magnesium, and other minerals and vitamins that ensure healthy bones, teeth, skin, and hair. You need to take your supplements on a full stomach to prevent nausea. When it comes to exercise, most Cancers prefer to dance, swim, or simply stroll along the beach. There is no reason for you to suffer for fitness.

You can be deliciously physically fit without destroying your personal and emotional health. Exercise is always best when it soothes your mind and opens your creative channels. Boot camp–style workouts have their place, but they aren't particularly sustainable in your busy life.

Just like Scorpio and Pisces, yours is a Water sign, known for absorbing the joy, sorrow, tension, and excitement occurring around you. Sometimes the intensity is too much. You feel anxious, nervous, scared. Most of you decide that drinking is a well-deserved and therapeutic activity after a stressful day. One drink turns into two pitchers—and so on. And of course, many of you have a hard time sleeping, so you consume more than the recommended dose of sleeping pills.

What is a lovable Cancer to do? For starters, be choosy but not isolationist when it comes to friends, men, and colleagues. Choose strong-willed friends that help you make smart health decisions instead of selecting a pack of enablers. No one is going to be your magical, perfect Tinker Bell. Everyone at one point or the other will fib, exaggerate, or misbehave.

Friends and Family

Astrologically, yours is the sign representing home, family, birth, breasts, the abdomen, the lining of the heart and lungs, and the swallowing mechanism. Cancer is associated with family traditions and memories (the scrapbook keeper who remembers everyone's birthday). Many of you have mixed emotions about having your own children. Your sisters' kids—great. Your best friend's kids—brats, but still no problem. You hesitate about having your own (what if something goes wrong?) and may worry yourself sick during pregnancy.

Spiritual astrologers point out that you're here to create your own version of an ideal family. That may be traditional or something resembling a tribe of like-minded friends. You can pretend to enjoy going it alone, but you need to realize that *no one* believes you're happy all by yourself.

Even before you started your period, you knew that being female is a big deal with a high emotional cost. You suffer when family members feud or holidays get ruined because of Uncle Larry's drunken temper tantrums or your favorite sibling runs away from home. The mere thought of a breakup or the destruction of the family unit is horrifying and shocking. You'd prefer things staying the same instead of falling apart, even when family members are utterly miserable. The known, as unpleasant and imperfect as it is, is easier to cope with than the big, hairy, fang-toothed unknown.

Until you personally experience the heart-wrenching despair of being in a marriage that's not working or a friendship that is so toxic that it's making you ill, you stubbornly cling to preserving "happily ever after" myths. It takes brutal honesty, lengthy tell-all hours in a therapist's office, and maybe a scary illness before you allow yourself to admit that yes—something needs to change.

Learn the lifesaving concept of acceptance. Accept people as they are. If you don't like their lifestyle or attitude, don't invite them into your inner circle. Practice acceptance by consciously detaching from circumstances that hurt you. When you don't interpret another's actions as personal, you can see things in a clear light. You also save yourself loads of worry, angst, and bouts of nausea and bloating. Acceptance is really worth learning.

Love

Eventually when the timing is just right, and trust has been earned during good and bad times, you allow another to get closer. Understand that intimacy and sex fall under different headings for you. Intimacy involves risk, heartbreak, putting your fragile faith and trust in another's hands. Sex is sex, often anonymous and physical with no expectation of a deep, long-lasting connection. Those of you with the most profound trust issues (due to emotional disappointment or loss at an early age) save yourself lots of time and drama and just name your vibrator "Geraldo."

Your perfect vision of the way things are supposed to be might not last, but that doesn't mean your relationship is ready for the dump or that you're a freaking failure. Wrap your sensitive little Crab heart around this: Every so-called flop is a valuable lesson. If you allow yourself to experience the fullness of the grieving process when a loss, embarrassing failure, or breakup occurs, you emerge much stronger and smarter than you were before.

You're likely to outgrow your first marriage, but not before having a child or two.

Cancer + Aries

Because neither of you is looking for easy, predictable pap, this match can work. Sure, there will be moments when you're ready to throttle your impulsive, enfant terrible Ram. At times you look at him and all you see is an angry child, mad at the world because his bike has a flat tire. This is one of those "can't live with or without" numbers. You know you're essential to his sexual needs. You also realize that he needs mothering and behavior modification. Maybe he felt neglected as a child or didn't measure up to his parents' great expectations. That's why your "come to Mama" warmth is so appealing to him. He is smitten with your body. He's an alpha male (complete with tormented teenage testosterone) and you're the essence of womanhood. He, to paraphrase Tom Cruise in *Jerry Maguire*, feels utterly completed by you. That doesn't mean he'll always be thoughtful and considerate. But it does suggest that he's a goner. Even if you decide you've had enough of his childish impatience and frustration and decide to dump him, he won't let you go without a fight (translation: drive-by episodes, lots and lots of them). Why? Because you, Crab Cakes, are his entire world.

The Bottom Line: The things that annoy you about him also endear him to you. He's got you on a pedestal as the mutha of all muthas. Even if you pack on the pounds, he finds you sexy, juicy, and very desirable. This is a high school romance that never ends. Tons of passion, jealousy, frustration, and intensity. You enjoy his Heathcliff sensitivity and rage. **Rating: ******

Cancer + Taurus

This is almost too easy. You both love food and learning new culinary tricks. You adore the luxury of sleeping in and lolling around in bed. You're both oral, sexually and otherwise, and believe that more is more. You both want a very comfortable home with a gadget-stocked kitchen, a bathroom luxe enough to live in, and cushy, comfy furniture. The bedroom is your favorite, for all the right reasons. You adore Taurus's Midas touch with money. His gift for attracting opportunities and masterminding the next big obsession or real estate venture actually excites you sexually. You really admire this man. You might not trust him entirely; he's so good-looking, so well-endowed, and so insanely popular, successful, and charming that you suspect everyone—even close friends—of trying to poach your man. So jealousy could (but doesn't have to) create friction. He might not worry too much about your extracurricular activities, but if he's twenty minutes late returning from his workout, your suspicion antennae sometimes poke up.

The Bottom Line: Scrumptious moments far outweigh jealous, insecure times. Drop the drama, work on your self-esteem, and invite the Bull into your life. When you're not fighting, being with this man is more fun than anything else you've ever done. This is a lifetime romance that only gets better, once you get your insecurity and his monogamy challenges under control. **Rating: *****

Cancer + Gemini

Ask anyone and they'll tell you that Gemini can be maddeningly disturbed at times, but never, ever boring.

Trouble is, you rather enjoy your pleasant, corny little routines. Gemini finds it quaint and adorable when he's wooing you, but quickly tires of your fears, your mom's morning calls, your food allergies, and most of the things that you're attached to. Gem loves to test the water and challenge your boundaries as frequently as possible. You feel pushed and slightly threatened by him. You also feel that he's talking down to you, as if he thinks your brain is feeble and half the size of his. Granted, he's smart and funny. He's very attractive, but he can also be a mental or emotional bully. You don't appreciate him rolling his eyes when you discuss family members' stories, holidays past, or even your childhood disappointments and victories. He views your past as old news. He's fascinated by what he views as more important pasts (bios of great leaders, conquests of continents, construction of cathedrals), so you feel marginalized. You begin to look at him as Mr. Smarty-Pants even when you're the one bringing in the most bacon every month. You feel like the foil for his mean jokes, bad examples, and ultimately questionable relationships.

The Bottom Line: This works nicely for some people but can devastate others. Make sure you keep your money separate and you retain control of the finances, deeds, and contracts, because eventually you wise up and leave Smarty-Pants behind. Your gentle psyche and sensitive emotions need support, not a continuous demolition process. This can work in special cases, but could be very tough on your self-esteem. **Rating: ***

Cancer + Cancer

Together you can create a connection as potent as a well-run nuclear power plant or devolve into a total meltdown that sends everyone heading for the hills. You're both touchy-feely types, easily wounded and known for your long memory for hurts, slights, and humiliations. Full moons, new moons, eclipses, and all manner of planetary activity affect you in ways that others seem less bothered by. If both of you are feeling wounded at the same time, *Houston— we have a problem*. But if your charts are just different and balanced enough so that you complement and calm each other's moods and fears, this can be magic. Moderation is a challenge. If your charts are complementary, you understand each other better than anyone else ever could and know exactly when to speak up or back off. The things that annoy you about him (his mommy issues, his menu choices, his smoking and drinking) probably mirror fears that you've held in your heart for years. You're stronger than he is. He, on the other hand, isn't quite "there" yet—but he can grow into a wiser man, perhaps with your help. It's your call, Cancer girl. If he looks like another burden for you, and his mother is a demanding beast, maybe you should pass. If he's trying hard, and his mom is friendly and appreciative of you, this is worth exploring.

The Bottom Line: So much depends on your charts and ability to grow, change, forgive, and take responsibility. If you're both grown-ups and willing to be accountable, this could be a perfect match. You can't rewrite his past or deeply ingrained habits. You can accept him as he is, or assist him in changes that he wants to make. This connection is megaintense—and sometimes, a true mate-for-life combination. **Rating: *****

Cancer + Leo

You enjoy Leo's panache, flattery, and robust love of good sex, great wine, and excellent hotel accommodations. You feel like a princess for a day—or however long this fling lasts. It could go on for years and years, mostly happy ones at that. Or you might start snooping around and discover details about his behavior and extracurricular activities that alarm you. Once you start doubting him about small things, big things usually follow. You're very psychic and have no difficulty reading his mind, once the hormonal haze of fresh lust/love burns off. Turns out he's got a routine, repeats a lot of the same sex chat, and tells every woman he's with that "this might be forever." Monogamy isn't Leo's specialty. He also has the screwball idea that you're there to service his special sexual needs. Sure, he spends a wad of cash in order to impress you—expensive champagne, room at the Ritz—but even that goes a little flat when it's clear that the room service gang know Mr. Leo, almost too well. At any rate, some of you weigh the pros and cons and decide this still rates high as a delicious fairy tale. For the rest of you, this fractured fairy tale is over long before your golden carriage changes back into a pumpkin.

The Bottom Line: The question this connection

poses revolves around truth, trust, and ethics. Can you ignore Leo's revolving flirtations and monogamy lapses? Are you willing to share him like a sex co-op? Chances are, the answer to both questions is no. You need to be able to trust your bedmate and alleged soul mate. Be careful with this one—he just might break your little Crabby heart. **Rating: ***

Cancer + Virgo

This really works. You understand each other, provide love and stability for one another, and over time, trust each other implicitly. You can glide into the future together, holding hands, sharing dreams, and reaching goals as a team of lovers, not rivals. You make excellent friends, largely because you respect each other's space, privacy, and preferences. There's a lot of maturity built into this pairing. Once the two of you get together, it's difficult to find a legitimate reason to be pried apart. In some ways, you feel as if you were separated at birth, even if there's a substantial age difference between you. The things you care passionately about are almost identical. You enjoy taking care of Virgo because he's so grateful for your love and attention. You adore being with Virgo because you always find something new and impressive about his view of the world, talent, or background. Most of all, you feel safe with Virgo. His word is solid. Each time he demonstrates that he's as good as the promise he makes, you feel more in love, achingly so. Children are likely. Maybe you'll have kids together, or perhaps one or both of you have a child from a previous relation-ship. You and Virgo are a strong team, create a healthy, fun home, and have lots of friends. This one is definitely a keeper!

The Bottom Line: Don't let go of Virgo. Once you two start talking, the conversation could last a lifetime. The crème de la crème of friendship and romance: an affair to relish and remember. **Rating: *****

Cancer + Libra

You're very attracted to Libra's style, personality, affa-bility, and humor. In many ways, he's as familiar and comfy as an old friend or family member. But in other ways, he leaves you feeling undernourished in the love and passion department. You're seeking the kind of man-woman attach-ment that defies legend, religious differences, and unfath-omable obstacles. In other words, he's just not hot enough for you. He looks hot, but his lovemaking (and foreplay) seems mechanical, furtive, and less than inspired. You're not looking for perfection; but by God, you are looking for authenticity—someone who would offer you his seat on a *Titanic* lifeboat. Libra isn't that guy. Sure, he's handsome and intuitively understands how to dress, smell, and behave in most circumstances. There's something missing—an unknown quantity that results in "whatever" instead of "whoopee." He's a living Ken doll that offers a presentable image but feels lukewarm and plastic when you need some sort of commitment or serious decision-making. And he's too easy to manipulate and push around, making it impossible for you to respect him. He's fine as a comfy old shoe, but not so much in the hot buttered love category.

The Bottom Line: It's true—sometimes familiarity breeds contempt. Don't you have something more important or interesting to do? Like pull weeds out in the garden? **Rating:** *

Cancer + Scorpio

You have officially entered the hot zone. This combo is jalapeño heaven stuffed with a Scotch bonnet. You two generate a lot of heat as a couple—and it isn't always friendly, but it is worth every stinging, singeing moment. You cannot resist each other's advances. You say and do things you normally wouldn't dare to. If you were brought up with gobs of guilt and shame, it goes *poof* when Scorpio presents his luscious, formidable stinger. This could be the best thing that's ever happened to you, as long as you're ready for biblical-scale drama, jealous rages, and mood swings. Revenge definitely plays a starring role in this hot stew of complications. You know going in that there might be a few problems—such as a maniac ex with a penchant for keying your car or slashing your tires, or a bankruptcy or two. Because you're so fabulously turned on, you tell your intuition to go to hell and decide to enjoy the ride. Well, you certainly learn a lot in this adventure. It can be stunning and magnificent, producing children, creative masterpieces, and an extended stay in the fast lane. Or it could dissolve into addiction, anger, unmet needs: a frozen Siberia. The desire and passion are initially irresistible. The question is, will it crash and burn? Or will it be handled with care and something in very short supply when you two get together: restraint?

The Bottom Line: Sometimes an attraction is too hot and chaotic to last. But this relationship could also be life changing for both of you. An attraction this strong deserves a high rating, whether it lasts or not. **Rating: ******

Cancer + Sagittarius

Sagittarius is a tough science project. Nothing he does makes sense to you, and yet you're oddly attracted to this strange, wild beastie boy of a man. Maybe his spontaneity excites and enamors you. Maybe you get a thrill up your spine from spending time with a certifiable bad boy—Brad Pitt before he got domesticated, Kiefer Sutherland, Jake Gyllenhaal, Billy the Kid—you get the picture. Or maybe it's that you enjoy having some of the hottest sex you've ever experienced (when he's not drunk or using). You feel protective of him and view him as a rebel with a cause but almost no common sense. That's what makes you so important to him. He needs you to gently, firmly rein him in, clean him up, teach him a few manners—and yet avoid crushing that wild streak that created all the magic in the first place. You might become a regular at codependent meetings, depending on how many times he slides off the wagon and gets into trouble (read: Kiefer Sutherland),

and learn a lot more about codependency than you ever thought possible. So much depends on his maturity level. Keep in mind that monogamy is a tough gig for him. That may never change—except for one very important point: He finds you utterly, maddeningly hot, sexy, and desirable. Just understand you might be taking on a load of excess baggage (unpaid parking tickets, maxed-out credit cards, and that kid he forgot to mention). You're strong enough to handle him. Question is—*do you want to?*

The Bottom Line: You and Mr. Sagittarius may argue a lot. He feels a need to rebel and be his own man. But he needs you to keep him out of trouble. He knows it, too. Might/might not be worth the struggle, effort, and tirades from Mr. Wild. But when it's good, it can be very, very delectable. **Rating: **

Cancer + Capricorn

This is a classic match, based on tradition, stability, security, shared values, and generally similar backgrounds. It lacks that je ne sais quoi prevalent in some of the other matches. But what it offers you (peace of mind, a real home, a position in the world, security) can make up for a joyride to nowhere. It really depends on your state of mind and priorities. If you're still kicking tires, trying to figure out what you want in a relationship, this might be too confining or mature. (If you need to sow some wild oats, find a Sagittarius. After you've bailed Sir Sagittarius out of jail a few times, Capricorn starts looking really good.) Capricorn seems older and wiser than his years. He might not be as spontaneous as some of the other guys, but he's very strong and sexy when the two of you are alone. This man can rock your world and give you a solid marble floor to stand on. He wants you to be happy, safe, and fulfilled. You may use different words to describe your dreams, but you almost always want the same things. There may be times when you need a girls' night out with some of your rowdy pals. Before the end of the evening, you'll be very glad to return to your protective, understanding Capricorn. This connection gets points for withstanding the test of time.

The Bottom Line: Once you and your Capricorn lower your defense shields and really connect, you might decide that you've found the perfect man. Of course, it doesn't hurt that Capricorn views you as the only woman he wants—forever. **Rating:** *****

Cancer + Aquarius

You're an odd couple, but this match can really last. Along the way, you'll be forced to examine your strengths and weaknesses, so metamorphosis occurs at regular inter-vals. This isn't an easy pairing, but it can be a great one, especially if you're ready to change your life and crank open your mind. Aquarius sets off mental bombshells that force you to examine habits, traditions, and accepted lifestyle choices that, until now, you were incurious about. When you're with the iconoclast of the zodiac (the guy who ques-tions everything: every rule and propped-up political figure or airhead celebutante), two things can happen. You can get scared and skedaddle, or you can share a big adventure that could last a lifetime. Each Aquarius seems to be a unique specimen, guaranteed to challenge accepted laws, rules, and standards and get everyone thinking, talking, and probably fighting. He might not be the most popular man you know, but he will be the most unforgettable. He may be abrasive at times, especially if he suspects someone is a lying, craven hypocrite. And he can be very stubborn—stubborn enough to leave a high-paying job because he doesn't agree with the company motto. Yes, Aquarius is eccentric, brilliant, and often a loner. (Sounds a little bit like you, doesn't he?)

The Bottom Line: At least give him a try. You'll never meet anyone identical to him again. You'll grow a lot, learn a lot, and become more confident because of your experiences with him. This pairing might take some getting used to, but it's potent enough to enhance your life and expand your spirit. **Rating: *****

Cancer + Pisces

As long as drugs and other addictions don't take over, this is an excellent match. You maintain most of the control: You handle the money, make the big-ticket decisions, and determine whether to buy a house in a certain location. Pisces may periodically disagree, but he generally defers to your expertise and budgetary skills. Pisces just wants to touch and be touched, and he loves, loves, loves you. And it's for real. This man thinks you're the most beautiful woman he's ever laid eyes on. He will write songs and poems and dedicate them to you. The sweetness and emotion is juicy and palpable, like perfectly ripe fruit. You need to follow up on this one because, addictions aside, it's pretty close to an ideal match. You share lots of rollicking sex, but you also have a powerful spiritual connection. You can feel when he's upset or in trouble, even if he's in another country. And he's the same way. You text or call each other at the same time, expressing undying love and concern. The other amazing thing about Pisces is that he is an imaginative chef. No matter how busy his day job, he loves to regale you with a special feast that he put together with his artistic imagination and gentle, loving hands. Speaking of hands, he's likely to offer you a relaxing après-dinner massage, which of course is followed by a dessert of passionate, heart-and-soul sex, far too yummy to pass up.

The Bottom Line: Pisces could be your dream lover, beautifully packaged and filled with wonder and magic. Give this connection some time to grow and develop. Looks like Sleeping Beauty just found her Prince! **Rating:** *****

What Does the Future Hold?

Saturn transits can be a bitch. Your next big Saturn cycle (all of them are important, but this one is extra important) occurs between the fall of 2012 and late December 2014. This one is all about making personal choices, such as whether to get married, get divorced, get close, have babies, or adopt babies. Very essential, life-changing decisions buzz about your brain during this stretch, and you feel every little bit of it.

The next big one starts in late 2017 and continues, haltingly, until the end of 2020. Whoa: This is a big one. You'll reload and reexamine a business and/or personal connection: Right? Wrong? Toxic? You may relocate to find better opportunities and people to live and interact with. Some of your elderly or sickly relatives may pass away. There's a feeling of "I'm pretty much on my own right now" that you gradually accept and grow from. But breaking your dependency on certain people, habits, and attitudes can simultaneously expand your options. Saturn teaches you to let go in order to get more. Yes: Saturn is paradoxical.

How to Interact with a Cancer

DO:

- Be considerate and kind about Cancer's quirks and dietary habits.
- Be polite, friendly, and respectful to Cancer's family members and lifelong friends. Don't make Cancer choose between you and a long-term pal.
- Respect Cancer's memories, traditions, and sentimental attachment to childhood toys, books, photos, and kitchen gadgets.
- Remember that Cancer is very sensitive and subject to stewing about unkind remarks for days, months,

or years. Think before making a joke at her expense, even if you think it's hilarious.

- Remember that Cancer is insecure about her appearance and weight and may be shy. Make things as comfy and relaxed as possible.

DON'T:

- Ever say a harsh word about Cancer's family members or close friends. Zip your lips when the urge hits.
- Make fun of family recipes that seem straight out of the fifties. They probably are, and Cancer loves them, so accept it.
- Separate Cancer from her hobbies, friends, or favorite sports. These are her lifelines.
- Ever betray her trust and faith in you. Once that's broken, it can't be fixed.
- Give away anything her family members have passed down to her. They may seem like junk to you, but they are special mementos to her.

Leo

♌

You, You, You

Is there anything more inviting than long, soft, silky hair, perfectly plumped lips, teeth whitened to showbiz standards, long slim legs, a round rump, and the bestest boobs money can buy?

Of course not.

But besides Leo's reputation of being a rich-husband thief and an attention-grabbing Lioness who causes more rear-end collisions than any other sign (especially in L.A., the capital of blond-tressed, dangerously territorial felines), Leos can be artistic, theatrical, good mommies, great mistresses, and fabulous shoppers on Rodeo Drive. Do a drive-by and see for yourself.

Leo, the fifth sign of the zodiac, is a Fire sign. Once you've felt the scorch of a Leo's love, possession, or disdain, you might need a surgeon to repair the damage. It's no accident that Leo is the fifth sign, either. Number five is the fun number—it says, Let's get tricked up like a

Playboy Bunny and attend a *fun*ction filled with influential, rich, powerful people who might give you a gift or a part in a straight-to-video (just a hair away from porn) flick. You are a proud opportunist and understand, like all people influenced by five and Fire, that life is all about the win.

And if the unexpected occurs and you don't win, you retain the right to sue or otherwise ruin the perp's reputation.

If you were born during the first ten days of Leo, you are a super-Leo, with noticeable Leo traits: passionate, proud, competitive, dramatic, possessive, and creative. If you were born during the second ten days of Leo, you possess Sagittarian traits, making you a freedom lover, a writer, a teacher, a person with strong spiritual beliefs, and a nature and privacy lover. If you were born during the final ten days of Leo, you take on Aries traits, emphasizing a strong "me first," "I'd rather do it myself," extremely competitive disposition.

You're also a proud member of the fixed signs: Taurus, Leo, Scorpio, Aquarius. This indicates that you will change your opinion only when extremely compelling evidence is offered. Even then, you might not budge. It also reveals your built-in tough-minded competitive nature. Fixed signs want to run things, even if it's from the background. Leos, of course, never run things from the background. Leos can't resist taking center stage. Don't pretend you didn't know that.

Once you get your claws into some form of juicy meat, you don't let go until you've had your fill. You *never, ever* give up. That brings up another one of your outstanding, fearsome qualities: You, Lioness, are a fixed sign. No one can change or rearrange anything about you without your approval.

Your sense of style is generally classic, except for your penchant for ornate rings, countless strands of gold that drip perfectly into your dewy décolletage, and hair that always looks done. Once you find a look that reflects the star that you are, you'll fight a stylist's suggestion to bring your look into a fresher, newer phase. You don't want anyone thinking you're trying too hard, even though you cannot stop yourself from being queen of any group you participate in.

Leo rules the heart. You're all heart when it comes to rescuing friends and wounded animals. You're full of heart and soul when it comes to crazy, passionate love that borders on obsession. You interpret art, communication, music, and colors by how much you love or hate them. While Cancers and Virgos trust their gut, you always trust your heart.

Beautiful, seductive, and predatory, these sleek jungle queens always walk away with the biggest prize—and sometimes it's someone else's husband (as long as he's rich and powerful enough).

Stars with your star sign: Angie Harmon, Charlize Theron, Emmanuelle Béart, Halle Berry, Hayden Panettiere, Hilary Swank, Jaime Pressly, Jackie Kennedy Onassis, Jennifer Lopez, Kate Beckinsale, and Madonna. Seriously, would any of you non-Leos have the nerve to arm-wrestle any of these kick-ass babes?

If You Were an Animal . . .

You'd be an untamed lioness, fiercer than your mate du jour and extremely protective of your offspring. If necessary—and for the sake of your kids and other loved ones—you have no problem committing violent acts that protect what you hold dear.

Career and Money

Although you're tough-minded and sacrificial enough to work three jobs on three hours of sleep a night in order to provide for your loved ones, you were not born to be humbled, humiliated, and disrespected by others far less gifted, sensitive, and strong.

During hard times, you wish you could be invisible because you're too broke to afford basic dental and medical care, not to mention decent clothing. When Dolly Parton's country classic "Coat of Many Colors" becomes your theme song, you know you're in trouble.

Many of you spend months or years in abusive, addictive relationships that caring friends try to pry you away from. You stick with a crappy situation as long as there's something to cull from it. Sound odd? It's part of your heart-centered creative need to grow from pain, pleasure, shock, neglect, and fear. Your dream is to overcome each obstacle with an overwhelming victory. In each challenge at work, home, or school, you repeatedly prove that you're so much more than others give you credit for.

You're proud—at least until you've had the crap kicked out of you a few times, been publicly humiliated (think of the messy Leo combo Bill Clinton and Monica Lewinsky), or gotten fired by a butt-smooching new hire with maybe 25 percent of your brain capacity. Getting past the hurt pride, anger, and humiliation opens your eyes to other talents, values, and hidden strengths you possess. And, Lioness, once your fierce mind is made up, nothing and no one can beat you to the finish line. You need to win, whatever it takes.

Ultimately, your career needs to provide the following: self-respect; security; food, shelter, and education for your brood; and the opportunity to explore vast layers of hidden talent (secreted in your heart like veins of gold). Gold, incidentally, is your favorite metal—and it looks amazing next to your polished skin when you call a meeting to order. You seek prestige—not from being born in some old-world manor, but from making your mark on a very rumpled, often crude world. You aim to civilize, educate, and raise awareness that anyone can move beyond humble beginnings and soar into a sparkling, unlimited universe of opportunity. This makes you a remarkable role model. Keep in mind that others are watching, taking notes, and mimicking your style and behavior.

Your life's work is to inspire and lead by example. You might become that marvelous teacher who unlocks the mystery behind certain learning disabilities, setting free creative minds and giving kids confidence to succeed. You might become a family therapist who has learned not merely from books and years of education, but also from living through years of personal pain and suffering. You are a powerful, magnificent survivor who others listen to and recognize as special but also "one of us." The more actively you engage with the world, the more likely you are to positively change the world. With a little extra effort, you can make a big impact.

Then, of course, there are the glam careers with outrageous salaries so bodacious that the zeros make your eyes cross. Some of you become famous pro athletes or tough but beloved coaches. Many of you choose to either photograph models or be a model. Your secret specialty is and always will be lighting. Acting, singing, dancing, and performance art all appeal to your Leonine roots. You often find that although the big dollars and rave reviews for your work come from grown-ups, you treasure the work you do with children and animals the most.

You tend to be lavish, especially if you come from very humble beginnings. One glance at your shoe, jewelry, and couture clothing collections explains it all. If you've fought your way out of poverty and into the big time, you're going to enjoy every last outrageous bit of it. Generous to a fault, some of you end up literally losing everything your sudden success and good fortune offered. This strongly suggests that you should protect yourself with the best-qualified, most reputable and conservative money managers possible. You also need to invest in stable, reliable, tangible things—like land.

Health

You'd much rather look slim and large breasted with a high, tight ass than dumpy and ordinary, so you're willing to engage in some unhealthy habits to get that Playboy-Bunny-on-steroids look (especially when you're young), like using laxatives and appetite suppressants, smoking like a chimney (even if you're asthmatic), and simply going without food until you take a tumble on the catwalk like Naomi Campbell. Even that won't stop a young, gritty Lioness from being the hottest iconic model of scary/sexy/skinny womanhood. The ravages of bad habits don't ever faze you (outside of accidents, overdoses, etc.) until you start seeing physical proof that you're not as smooth and sleek as you once were. Sure, surgery is useful, but temporary.

Refocus, Lady Lion. It's not your appearance that makes or breaks your health, quality of life, or longevity. Your formidable look may be dramatic, but it's an illusion. It's your cardiovascular system that you need to zoom in on, especially if you have a family history of heart disease, stroke, aneurism, or vascular problems. Keep your mighty heart healthy by getting regular blood work that tracks your cholesterol, triglycerides, and other indicators affecting your heart. Remember, Leo: When it comes to you, it's all about the heart.

Friends and Family

Ah, yes . . . ye olde saw about blood being thicker than water. Guess that depends on who you've got for friends and family members. For many of you, nothing is more important than family. But for a lot of you, what really boosts your mood, opens your mind, and makes life worth living are your unconditionally caring, loving friends. They never stop surprising you with sincere kindness and generosity.

You love babies, human and animal. You're a snuggly cuddler, just like they are. It's a perfect fit. But you also love nannies and grannies who rush to the rescue and make it possible for you to run a few errands, see a movie, or do something unspeakably, spontaneously sexy. And lucky you: Your closest pals keep secrets.

You even enjoy being around a friend's teenage kids. You're not threatened by their independence and find it refreshing and exciting. You communicate with other people's kids more as a friend than as an adult.

Although you tend to idealize what a perfect relationship or family life is like, you still believe that family life is sacred and timeless. Holidays are always huge events (squabbles and all) when you're involved. During big celebrations and holidays, your home is the epicenter of Party Central. You take pride in sharing your favorite food, champagne, and lavish desserts with treasured friends and family members. An invitation from you means a lot.

Love

The phrase "in love with love" was coined especially for you, Ms. Leo. You adore romance, flirting, and the rush you get from making a grand entrance in a fabulous, body-hugging dress. You enjoy having your picture taken, especially when you're trying to impress a new man or attempting to make an ex jealous. Actually, you're so glam that you make a lot of people jealous—even a few of your peeps.

Passion can make or break a love connection. Sometimes, you care so deeply and are so fiercely territorial that you scare or intimidate a man. Other times, you give so much of yourself that you're in danger of being used or taken for granted. It's so difficult to find the perfect balance.

You test a potential mate, just to see how manly and strong he is. In your heart of hearts, you want a strong man who is confident enough to trust, worship, and remain madly in love with you.

The contrast between dating and living together can be disappointing and chip away at your dreamy romantic desires. You need attention, respect, and loads of love. Make sure the man you choose is up to the job—and passionately in love with you. Don't settle for less.

Leo + Aries

Both of you are total smarty-pants types, and you make nearly perfect sparring partners. Since each of you is always right and the other one is always just plain stupidly wrong, this argumentative connection (we could call it a lifelong debate) could linger for years and years. No two people can talk a subject to death and disagree on so many details better than you, which is the primary reason you're either invited to dinner parties and other shindigs—or not. The flirting factor heats up after a few sips of Kahlua, and then you and Aries perform a pretty good version of *Who's Afraid of Virginia Woolf?*—scaring some guests and entertaining others.

The Bottom Line: Drama queens eat this up and ask for seconds. People who enjoy peace and tranquility find that it increases their need for antianxiety meds. Just how much shouting do you enjoy during the course of a day? This connection is a loud fight to the finish. **Rating: ****

Leo + Taurus

As improbable as this blend sounds, it makes the mercury rise, maybe not fast enough for Leo but just right for Taurus. Leo might bitch about how stubborn and cranky and perpetually late Taurus is. Then Leo gets even by arriving at an important event two or more hours into the ceremony. Game on! There can be spiteful moments and a war of the wills, but everything changes when the subject of sex comes up. Taurus is as good as it gets in the attraction department. Taurus not only understands how to coax a woman into bed, and generate multiple orgasms (his specialty), he also knows how to make tons of money. The kind of money that buys all those baubles, bangles, and beads that Leos love. The kind of money that sends Leo's children to the best private schools, while Taurus and Leo enjoy luxurious travel excursions. What's not to love?

The Bottom Line: The rumor is that push-up bras were invented by a Taurus man. So show him what you've got. This connection is very physical, acquisitive, and tantalizing. If you let this one slip through your fingers, it might be time to resume your meds. **Rating: *****

Leo + Gemini

You two are hilarious. Sure, you're competitive and sarcastic, but you usually make up for bad behavior by presenting your Gemini with a bauble or a rollicking sexual experience. You both talk a lot, have very specific, graphic sexual fantasies, and love, love, love gossip—any kind of crazy, mean Hollywood dirt is entertaining, true or false. As loose lipped as you can be, you can also be profoundly bookish and seek quiet little inns with fireplaces and big leather chairs and sofas to lounge and cuddle on. People with such remarkably active (often anxious) minds sometimes need to retreat from the world in order to find privacy and balance. This connection could last through almost any storm because you're both resourceful, in love, and supportive of each other.

The Bottom Line: I hear wedding bells. I even hear big anniversary bashes and commitment vows in the future. Some Leos have all the luck. . . . **Rating: *****

Leo + Cancer

You really try hard to find something fun, exciting, and interesting about Cancer. You try and try and try. At times, he's so sweet and thoughtful, hinting at a future together, maybe meeting his family (that probably includes an ex and a couple of kids), but something is just plain missing in this pairing. It's hard to put your finger on exactly what it is, but it may be his dull conversation. That's the good news. The bad news is that you don't trust him. If there were ever a time for you to put down that flute of champagne and think about what you're getting yourself into, it's now. You may or may not be sexually compatible. This isn't a total deal killer, but it certainly isn't a selling point. You probably will never know the real story behind his past drug, legal, or marital issues. Truth is, you're stronger, more honest, and more ambitious than he'll ever be. You don't respect him.

The Bottom Line: How fast can you run away from this guy? Ready, set, *go!* **Rating: ***

Leo + Leo

Aside from the opinionitis virus that permeates this combo, especially when you're with in-laws or are forced to spend long stretches of time in close proximity with each other, you do understand one another. *Maybe too well.* You know exactly how to squirt kerosene on his sparking insecurities. You can read him like a comic book and know when you've pushed too hard or have been too blatant or harsh. You can really grow from this relationship, despite the hair-raising hissy fits, the vanity issues, and your need for your own private bathroom and preening area. You love to be romanced and treated like a queen (after all, you are the queen!), but he likes to be treated like a queen, too—and there's the rub. You both need to learn a little bit about sharing, giving, and sacrificing for the health and longevity of your relationship. Sharing and sacrifice are tough sells for you. What you think is sacrifice is just normal daily life for others. The two of you make a huge entrance, love to laugh loudly, and adore big parties, bawdy jokes, and bragging about yourselves, your kids, and the famous people you know.

The Bottom Line: This is a mirror held to truth. You see so much of yourself in him—even the parts you despise about yourself. You might not last forever, but you will have a great time social climbing together—unless, of course, you're competing with each other. **Rating: ****

Leo + Virgo

You like Mr. Virgo. You can see real possibilities in him. Sometimes he's a bit stuffy, but you're better than anyone at loosening him up (as long as the doors are locked and the drapes are drawn). You understand Virgo's fascination with fantasy and periodic craving for a little friendly discipline among friends. You don't judge him in the classical sense—only in the theatrical sense, which of course drives Mr. Guilt Trip right off the mountainside into your tunnel of love. Some women are turned off by sexual games, but you love them—especially when it comes to humbling an otherwise very proud man into a quivering, electrified sexual power tool. Of course, you control the power, speed, volume, and frequency. When you're not spending stellar evenings in posh hotels, you make quite an impressive business duo, too. No wonder there is so much heat, drive, and energy pulsating from the two of you.

The Bottom Line: You always lick your lips and get a glint of mischief in your eyes, just thinking about Mr. Virgo. Quite possibly the hottest love affair you'll ever enjoy. Monogamy can be terribly difficult to maintain in this hot little thriller, but it's worth it. Sometimes pleasure and pain are inseparable. **Rating: ******

Leo + Libra

You genuinely enjoy Libra's conversation, humor, gentle smile, and willingness to have fun. You're all about fun, parties, family, and friends—and, OMG, Libra is, too! Could this be the perfect man? Well, actually, *yes*—he might be Mr. Right. You communicate in so many adorable ways with each other. Some of your friends might think you're lovesick loons, but who cares? You're having a great time with the guy you might spend your forever with. One thing the two of you do that annoys some friends and family members (and literally gags others) is your habit of baby-talking to each other. Although your cutesy-poo stuff might not fly with everyone, it apparently works wonders for the two of you.

The Bottom Line: Baby Libra wants to nurse Mama Leo. Rockabye Baby has never felt so good. **Rating: *******

Leo + Scorpio

This seems like an odd blend—party animal versus privacy freak—but it can work out quite nicely. You get hot under the collar just thinking about Scorpio's passionate, piercing looks that say, "Bedroom—*now!*" Scorpio can say so much without raising his voice or issuing a threat. You love a man like that: someone so confident and sure of the outcome that he already knows he's won. You can't fall fitfully in love with anyone who's not able to outsmart, outmaneuver, and overpower you. That's why Scorpio is so difficult to understand but impossible to keep your paws off. He can beat you at your own game. What a freaking turn-on! There will be battles—some may draw blood; others will leave years of simmering resentment and anger. But no one else will ever thrill you the way Scorpio does. And he knows it.

The Bottom Line: Don't even try to fight it. Give in and feel like a real woman for the first time in your life. Although this is sensationally sexy, it's also "War and Peace." Is it worth it? No doubt. **Rating: ******

Leo + Sagittarius

You two have big belly laughs and get into so much trouble together—especially when you're on the loose, traveling around anyplace but your hometown. You liberate each other and have a mutual desire for new experiences, foreign lands, antiquities, exotic cultures, and forbidden practices. You might get into a few wild situations that you

just narrowly escape with your pants, ID, and other personal property. Whatever you do, you're friends, first and
foremost. You might become lovers, too. Even if you don't
remain lovers due to inevitable infidelity, you can still be
pals. In fact, you're kind of like a comedy act. Just one or two
looks or words from him send you into a fit of uncontrol-
lable laughter. He's your walking, talking whoopee cushion.
Another thing that attracts you is your mutual fascination
with mystery, unique religious practices, and sacred places.

The Bottom Line: Love each other as great friends
with grand stories to tell. This connection can hold its own,
with or without sex and romance. This is an endearing
friendship that could last a lifetime. **Rating: ★★★**

Leo + Capricorn

Capricorn is probably someone you met through work
or while you were shopping or running errands. What
struck you first about Capricorn was his outstanding appearance. The next thing you noticed was the shape and size
of his hands and how gallant he was—opening car doors,
lifting boxes, going out of his way to make life easier for
you. He wooed you. He made you feel wanted, special, and
spectacular. All the other guys suddenly seemed so infan-
tile, weak, and (let's admit it) repulsive. Right away, you
thought, "We'd make beautiful babies." It's this kind of
passion and thought process that guarantees your relationship will move faster than anticipated. In fact, you might
find yourself pregnant before you've actually discussed

marriage. You'll always feel worshipped by Capricorn and know that you are not only loved, but are placed on a pedestal. Capricorn might not always be an easy guy to live with (he can be moody and pessimistic), but you'll never doubt that he'd do anything for you and will love you with every fiber in his body.

The Bottom Line: He might not be as sociable or glamorous as you, but he's a slave to your love, baby. You're the only woman in the world that matters. His worshipfulness of you lights up excitement, sexual tension, and magnificent compatibility. **Rating: ******

Leo + Aquarius

Direct opposites, you can complement and complete each other at times; and then there are those icy moments, crippled by stress and misunderstanding, when you don't even seem to speak the same language. There's plenty of fire and ice here. You provide the fire, while intellectual, often distant, hard-to-get Aquarius serves up lots of unavailable icy mystery. No matter how sophisticated you are, you view Aquarius as a worthy prize and challenge. Aquarius's eccentric, metrosexual looks add to your fascination. Plus, he rubs elbows with a great many writers, actors, performers, and designers. His world fascinates you, giving you access into unfamiliar surroundings that attract and push you away at the same time. You may be better friends than lovers. Your taste for romance can be too hot and hands-on for Aquarius to enjoy.

The Bottom Line: Hot and cold together generally produces a tepid environment. Yes for a party date (and even that's iffy)—no for a lover. **Rating: ***

Leo + Pisces

You see Pisces' luminescent eyes and fall into a trance that you never, ever want to pull out of. This is so powerful that it feels like a love addiction. You'd sell you soul for a weekend with Pisces, despite his reputation as a womanizer, boozer, druggie, or liar. He's just so hopelessly sexy, adorable, and charming—and, when he's not using, a phenom in bed. Your mentally organized friends, who are able to stand back and size up this unholy alliance, try hard to talk some sense into you—to no avail. You are insatiable for Pisces. Could this be dangerous? Sure, depending on his lifestyle, friends, and the situations he puts you in. The two of you are artistic, inspired souls and a lot more sensitive than most people realize. You are in a state of ecstasy when you're in the arms of your Pisces. If the two of you can turn your natural penchant for transformation into something transcendent, far beyond mere feel-good highs, you both have what it takes to help rebuild lives, return to health, and grow into confident happiness.

The Bottom Line: Not for the timid, conservative, or highly addictive. You'll earn every orgasm and spiritual realignment you get during this relationship. Big risks sometimes produce the grandest rewards. If you're tough enough and in love enough, go for it. **Rating: ****

What Does the Future Hold?

Until 2012, Neptune continues to play crafty shell games with your most important relationships. You need to make sure someone is who he or she claims to be before passing on any important information. You also need to avoid taking relationships at face value. Tend to another's needs. Show more interest. Be the one that he or she calls first.

Between 2011 and 2019, a large number of you will relocate, maybe to another country, and change the way you do business and communicate. Many of you will change your approach to education, emphasizing quicker ways to acquire knowledge that are also portable. If you wear glasses or contacts, anticipate that new medical and technical advances will change and improve vision.

How to Interact with a Leo

DO:

- Make positive remarks about Leo's mane, however sparse or dry it is.
- Give Leo a prepaid gift certificate to a spa or dermatologist.
- Send a birthday card—a real one, not a lazy-assed e-card—on Leo's birthday.
- Show an interest in Leo's kids, friends, pets, and hobbies. This is one of the quickest ways into a Leo's

heart. Remember that Leo's kids, friends, pets, and hobbies are an extension of Leo.

- Make a special effort to schedule lunches and/or evenings out, just to keep each other up-to-date on the latest gossip, thrills, men, and who's getting what done at the cosmetic surgeon's facility.

- Return calls. Leos need to be acknowledged and respected. If you're too busy for that, you don't have what it takes to be friends with Leo.

DON'T:

- Make disparaging remarks about Leo's hair, body, or clusters of conflicting jewelry.

- Criticize Leo's choices in male or female friends or companions.

- Offer advice unless it's requested. Even then, be kind and discreet and err on the side of compassion.

- Create heartache by repeating a cruel remark one of her alleged friends said about a Leo.

- Forget to introduce Leo to all your friends at parties and gatherings—especially the powerful ones that Leo so admires.

- Perpetually ask for money, favors, or special treatment from Leo. Don't put Leo in the embarrassing position of having to say no to a friend.

♌

Virgo

AUGUST 23–SEPTEMBER 22

♍

You, You, You

You're complicated. Filled with repressed longing and brimming with passion, ambition, and, most of all, an abiding need to maintain control of everyone nearby. You shudder at the thought that if anyone accidentally read your mind, they probably wouldn't like you. You set the bar incredibly high for yourself, and feeling inadequate is a regular occurrence.

It takes decades (and usually a great therapist and loyal, hardheaded pals who stand by you no matter what) for you to make peace with yourself and accept that you're a worthy, wonderful, highly competent, loving person.

You were born with doubts—lots of them. Your existential angst started in third grade and never quite climaxed. You don't want it to, and you put off that date with destiny by proving your personal right to live on planet earth every day. You stay busy. The busier you are, the less likely you are to ponder the powerful, terrible, wonderful universe within your busy little being. Unlike your surrounding signs (Leo and Libra) you don't believe you're entitled to anything. You believe you must do penance for each pearl of caviar or Birkin bag you can get your hands on. And finding the perfect mate? That takes even more hard work and sacrifice, which may explain why so many of you select men with baggage and adjustment issues. You adore fixer-uppers. You religiously, obsessively produce quality work, mending others' bodies and minds and straightening up your desk as well as others', and pray that God or Ganesh will notice.

Because you need to be in control, you're busy all the time. There are always needy people clustering around you, with multitudes of problems that they can't or won't deal with. You volunteer big fat slabs of time trying to make others happy, even when they've immunized themselves against joy. Eventually, you feel as joyless as the people you're trying to rehab and rescue. You acknowledge that it's a tiresome, thankless bore picking up another's mess, making excuses for friends who can't make it in to work, and accepting blame so that someone else doesn't have to. You start to realize that without you, a number of people you've propped up wouldn't be where they are today. This is the beginning of your transformation from grateful footstool to hot-blooded Queen Elizabeth I.

When it dawns on you that others actually believe that you can be replaced, you begin a lifelong toughening-up process. You get smart and start asking for more money, more respect, and more freedom (which, of course, you've earned with triple-digit interest). Your requests may not be granted, but your change of consciousness elevates your self-respect and a deepening well of core power. You're a powerful force in the making—and Goddess knows you've paid dearly for this lesson.

You need to feel valued, and until you learn to value yourself, you sell tiny lots of your heart, soul, time, happiness, and future in order to win another's love, attention, loyalty, or assistance. Remember, yours is an Earth sign, big on transactions: *If I give you this, then you give me that.*

The first ten days of Virgo fall squarely under the decanate of Virgo, giving those of you born then supreme Virgo status. Congratulations! The second ten days of Virgo fall under the decanate of businesslike Capricorn, giving you sharklike negotiation skills and persistence that shock your opponents. The third and final ten days of Virgo fall under the decanate of lovebug Taurus—pure, 100 percent U.S. prime, baby. You're extremely sensual, sexual, and irrepressible. You might be wearing a business suit, but your lingerie is totally naughty.

Your is one of the lusty, "touch me" triad of Earth signs, made up of Virgo, Taurus, and Capricorn. You like to feel, touch, and hold things before you buy them. You like valuables to be in the right place. It makes life so much simpler and less stressful. Only another Virgo can truly understand this.

You're also a wild and crazy member of the mutables: Gemini, Virgo, Sagittarius, and Pisces. Maybe not the most consistent people in the zodiac, but only because of annoying life interruptions. You know how it works: You hate to disappoint, so you agree to plans that screw up your schedge. Eventually you're smashed against the wall and can't possibly honor all the promises you've made. So you hate yourself. Typical mutable behavior.

Because you're a die-hard rescuing, quality-control, perfection-just-ain't-good-enough kind of gal, you struggle with the meaning of life, pretty much on a daily basis. "Why the hell am I here? Why am I not perfect, taller, thinner, richer, smarter, and utterly adored?" You bash your head against wall after wall, trying harder than just about anyone else to work magic on people and situations that refuse to cooperate. Darling: *Stop trying so hard*.

Stars with your star sign: Blake Lively, Raquel Welch, Heidi Montag, Nicole Richie, Sophia Loren, Jada Pinkett Smith, Salma Hayek, Cameron Diaz, Beyoncé, and Claudia Schiffer.

If You Were an Animal . . .

You'd undoubtedly be a graceful, dignified sandhill crane, who mates for life, fiercely guards its young, and covers unbelievable distances to select the best nesting places. Sandhill cranes are quality and safety conscious and believe in location, location, location—just like you.

Career and Money

Many of you are extremely creative and musically inclined. Because you know that no one can exceed your high standards, you're better off running your own business than being a tiny bureaucrat in a huge bureaucracy. In search of the finest quality, you may construct a specialized recording studio, manage a recording artist, or produce the finest musical instruments available.

You also have a keen interest in health, medicine, and cutting-edge surgical intervention, so a lot of you become doctors, therapists, or nurses. Viruses are particularly interesting to you. You want to know why viruses (good or bad) occur (is cancer a viral disease, and why do some people get it and others don't?) and how to prevent or contain an outbreak.

You're a stickler for organization, sky-high standards, excellent service, and on-time delivery. You can be a very demanding boss, tough on your staff, but your customers love you. They know that you'll always make good on your guarantees.

Be very cautious in business and finance. Just because an investment adviser comes highly recommended doesn't mean he won't make mistakes that erase half of your savings. Keep an eye on how your money is handled. Don't hesitate to squawk when you see something on a report or invoice that doesn't make sense. Ask questions and don't hesitate to move your money elsewhere if you aren't being treated respectfully and honestly.

Health

It begins inside. That's where all the magic, wonder, potential, and excellence are. Why do you think your digestive system is such a battleground? It's not just all the chocolate you eat. It's also that you can barely stomach some of the situations (and relationships) you've put yourself in.

And how about those headaches and sinus issues?—and don't forget the allergies. Could they be warning signs from your overstressed body asking you to stop clogging up your life with other people's mistakes and baggage? Yes!

You can work on awareness now or wait until you're one hundred years old. Chances are, you'll live a long time. You can make those years punishing or pleasurable by the choices you make.

The point, Goddess Virgo, is that you're stronger than most people. You have more to offer but cling to that vestigial response of hemorrhaging favors, money, time, love, and energy for people who haven't earned the right to be in your presence. It's time to trade up—and, if necessary, fake it until you can feel your bodacious power and goddess within.

You benefit from a calm, soothing environment. Sometimes you have no choice about the environment you find yourself in. Most of the time you do; so select friends, workplaces, shopping areas, and special areas in your home that offer the most peace and privacy. You're too sensitive and easily distracted to cope with unnecessary noise, tension, and pollutants.

Because of your sensitive nature, you may find that exercising at home is cleaner, less noisy, and less angst inducing than heading to a gym. You're disgusted by a smelly gym

with dubious ventilation and sweat-covered, poorly maintained equipment. Work out at home.

Friends and Family

You've felt responsible for your parents' and siblings'
happiness since your early childhood. With each passing
year, you pile more friends (and obligations) onto your aching shoulders. For some reason, you suspect that you had
something to do with their problems. It doesn't take much
for you to feel shame or disappointment with yourself when
there is a slight risk that you may have let down a friend or
family member. You'd rather chew off your own foot than
hurt a family member's feelings. Even the thought of it is
unbearable.

Extremely protective of friends and loved ones, you
may put yourself at risk while defending or watching out
for nieces, nephews, or Grandma and Grandpa. A strong
sense of duty and obligation is tattooed onto your soul.
You cannot rest until you're convinced that everyone is fed,
happy, healthy, and safe. That's a tall order.

To make things even more difficult, you insist that
things are done right and on time. Before you even get
started on a good deed, you're already in panic mode,
worried that you might screw up or disappoint someone. Most of the time, the only person who gets disap-
pointed is you. You expect so much of yourself—far more
than your friends or family do. They're so grateful just to

have you around. You've got to start acknowledging your good qualities, instead of obsessing about your mistakes. You are an extremely compassionate person who needs to be more protective about your own needs, feelings, and comfort.

Instead of making excuses for friends or relatives who say rude or insulting things to you, speak up. Tell them that anytime you feel the need for their comments and opinions, you'll ask for them. You'll score a self-respect victory for yourself and shock the rude insulter into silence.

Love

You believe in idealized romantic love. Heart-pounding movies, music, stories, and locations where legendary trysts occurred thrill you. As breathless and exciting as movies and stories are, your first love (the one you can't erase from your mind or get over) is even more intense. When you decide to give your heart to someone, it's a very big deal. You know you're taking the risk of being hurt but are so swept up in the moment that you bravely push ahead.

Most of the time, you're wary, observant, and even dismissive of someone who doesn't meet your lofty standards. The only exception to this is when you fall crazy in love. You suspend doubt when love hits you like a baseball moving at 140 miles an hour. All of your careful plans are put on pause. Because you are so willing to give up everything for the man you love, you must be especially careful about the man you choose. Make it easier on yourself by not spending time with people that you know have more problems than you do. Be leery of men who depend on you. Most people do depend on you. Dependency, however, isn't particularly romantic once the honeymoon is over.

Remember that peace of mind and a healthy, calm environment are essential to your mental health and emotional/physical balance. Do not rush into a romance with someone who needs you more than you need him.

Virgo + Aries

This is a growth connection that stimulates and eventually *forces* change, challenge, and enhanced self-awareness. This isn't a roll-over-and-play-dead connection—it includes jealousy, secrets that ultimately surface, and, yes, shockingly hot passion. It can work, but isn't for sissies. Initially, it's all love and hate and sex: a combustible magic. If you can weather the storms and extremes, you can settle into a remarkably stable "you and me against the world" blend. I happen to love this combo.

The Bottom Line: Sex, power, transformation, heat, more sex, and, ultimately, a better you. This pairing has a high heat factor. **Rating: ******

Virgo + Taurus

Forget all the homilies you've heard about this being a perfect match. It can be, but it can also be difficult. You will not tolerate cheating unless you're so smitten and passionate about someone that you refuse to give him up (see Virgo + Aries). Bulls tend to mosey around, looking for easy, available, fun sexploits. Their generous libido doesn't mean they don't find you attractive, but it might undermine your notoriously fragile self-esteem. Be really careful about getting involved with a Bull in a hands-on profession (doctor, teacher, or anything connected to travel). The issue is that once a Bull strays and gets away with it, it could easily turn into a lifestyle. This is heaven or hell, depending on your situation.

The Bottom Line: Remove the rose-colored glasses, wear a flak jacket, and approach with caution. **Rating: ****

Virgo + Gemini

Both of you are skittish, detail-obsessed, and easily annoyed by stupidity and noise pollution, so you definitely agree on what's wrong with the world and everyone else. Although old-timers warn against this pairing, it can work out very nicely—provided that each of you has your own fulfilling life, friends, money, and hobbies. If one of you is dependent or clingy, this connection goes the way of dust bunnies: into the trash. (But honestly—when is a Virgo or Gem clingy? Most of the time, you're high-strung and specialize in clever ways to quickly detach from dependent, agonizingly needy types.) Speaking of detachment, you can help each other (in a kind of cosmic twelve-step way) to stop saying yes to psychic vampires who want to slurp up your last bit of energy and time. Actually, as unlikely as this combo may seem, it can really work. Once you get to know each other, you almost feel as if you were separated at birth.

The Bottom Line: There will be heated debates on who is smarter or has full veto power, but you kind of dig that master/slave montage. **Rating: *****

Virgo + Cancer

Cancer loves for you to listen to his dreams, schemes, and what he views as brilliant ideas. You help him move beyond his comfortable "me" zone into something more community minded. You introduce him to people he'd probably never strike up a conversation with if it weren't for your helpful (translation: insistent) prompting. You see this as a science project with a future (marriage) and civilize and socialize him. You can make mad, passionate love and have heated debates, then kiss and make mad, passionate love again. This combo is fascinating because it evolves in unexpected ways. Initially, one of you is the alpha dog. Over time, the other one takes over. Now that's balance!

The Bottom Line: Your hopes and dreams can be thrillingly realized in the arms of a Cancer. You feel safe, secure, and cherished. **Rating: *******

Virgo + Leo

You probably share a number of favorite things, even though you cringe when Leo has one too many and performs an embarrassing floor show. Never one to call attention to yourself, you try to remain cool and detached while your Leo date flirts with virtually everyone and accuses you of being a dreary prude. Yes, you have some shared passions, but the way you interact with the world is very different. You don't *need* to be the center of attention or have the last arrogant, sloppy-drunk word. But Leo does. You might go ten long rounds with your rake of a man, but you'll finally lose respect for him in the end. This one requires a third party: a strong-willed couples therapist and possibly some medication.

The Bottom Line: Leo's self-absorption and self-indulgence stop being exciting and start feeling annoying. You can tolerate a lot, but even you know when it's time to bail. **Rating: ****

Virgo + Virgo

Well, stranger things have happened and succeeded. You both need to respect each other's space and privacy, and above all, *never* furtively rummage through each other's private papers, books, pictures, or e-mail. For starters, you might see something you really don't want to see. Second, trust is a megawatt issue for both of you. If either of you crosses that line or snoops around in the other's private stuff, there will be hell to pay. If you happen to discover old love letters or photos of a former girlfriend, you'll be livid with jealousy, no matter how emotionally secure you think you are. You won't be able to hold in the resentment and suspicion, so you'll drop hints until he finally figures out that you've been spying, eavesdropping, or snooping. That's one of the classic ways to lose a Virgo. Respect each other's privacy. It's a deal breaker if you don't.

The Bottom Line: If you love and respect yourself, this works. If you're not quite there yet, this has "Do Not Enter" plastered all over it. **Rating:** ***

Virgo + Libra

You enjoy Libra's social finesse and appreciation of the finer things in life. You sometimes feel that Libra doesn't understand responsibility or accountability to the extent that you do. But who does? You were born feeling responsible for original sin, and tend to tote that burden like a Sherpa most of your life. Libra lightens things up and seduces you into funny peccadilloes that almost always involve impulsive spending, luxury items, and hotel bar tabs. Libra encourages you to stop saying, "No, I really couldn't," and coaxes you to say, "Well, maybe just one." This might last, might not, but it's likely to be loads of fun while it does.

The Bottom Line: A little fun won't kill you and might make you ecstatically happy. Give this one a try. **Rating:** ****

Virgo + Scorpio

You two can talk about almost anything. Some of you successfully balance being business partners while still maintaining a lifelong friendship. You think in a similar fashion and are detail obsessed. Born to be critics of art, restaurants, fashion, and theater, you enjoy evenings out together, but really adore your privacy and beloved routines at home. Neither of you is especially receptive to drop-in visitors. You do your best to behave and be polite but can't wait for the pests to disappear. Then you can get back to your very private sultry lives. This one, with or without sex, is a bond that could last a lifetime—a unique, timeless connection held together with respect, love, and shared beliefs.

The Bottom Line: You fall in love with each other's mind and respect each other's space and eccentricity. Outsiders often don't understand your relationship—as if you care. That's why they're called outsiders. **Rating: *******

Virgo + Sagittarius

This one is a challenge, but if you're willing to detach a bit and not attempt to control Sagittarius's wandering eye or need to hang with old friends you don't approve of, it could work. Sagittarius loves excess. Consider for a moment a few famous Sagittarians—Anna Nicole Smith, Jimi Hendrix, and Jim Morrison—and you'll recognize that moderation isn't usually part of a Sagittarian lifestyle. Can you cope with that? If you're up for occasional adventurous hiking, biking, or climbing excursions and don't mind spending hours or days alone while he's out finding himself and not staying in touch, you'll do fine. You have different worldviews. For example, behaviors that you view as selfish seem normal and natural to him. He might describe those same behaviors as freedom. Just understand what you're getting into—and don't plan on rewiring or civilizing him. Won't happen in this lifetime.

The Bottom Line: You might think he's house-broken and trainable, but think again—and then move on. **Rating:** *

Virgo + Capricorn

You're both Earth signs and have a very special, tactile, intimate bond. You delight in each other's company. Each of you is privately shy and insecure, no matter how success-ful or famous you might be. All of your collective accom-plishments seem like child's play compared to the risk (and treasure) of exploring intimacy. Generally, you start out as friends—maybe working on a project together or working out at the gym together. Then you meet for coffee, lunch, a movie. And pretty soon you can't stay away. Give this deep, important connection lots of time to grow and develop. Although you sense that you're perfect for each other, you mustn't rush. Allow trust and confidence to grow—and then gun the engines.

The Bottom Line: You're in this for love and forever. **Rating:** *****

Virgo + Aquarius

This isn't an easy match, but each of you can get some-thing out of it even if it doesn't last. Aquarius benefits the most because he finds you so mysterious, sexy, intellectually stimulating, and more tempting than a hot fudge sundae. You, on the other hand, view Aquarius as a bad little boy who needs lots of behavior modification, a few hygiene lessons (ugh!), and some essential style tips. (Seventies fashion was okay in the olden days, but get out of those zigzag polyester stretch slacks—*now!*) If anyone can shape up an eccentric Aquarius trapped in a time warp, it's you. You'll learn a lot, and have plenty to laugh about, but are likely to lose interest long before Aquarius does.

The Bottom Line: When your work is done, you're *done* with him. **Rating: ****

Virgo + Pisces

As long as you're willing to assume most of the responsibility and control (music to your ears!), this can work very well. Just understand that Pisces may think he's ready to take action, to lead or be the decider, when in fact he's not. Luckily you're locked, loaded, and faultlessly prepared. You never look for excuses to avoid responsibility. That's Pisces' job. In fact, you make it easy for Pisces to play "Baby wants Mama now" for years to come. You both seem to enjoy this game—a lot. As peculiar as it sounds, this connection really works. You balance each other very nicely, providing the ballast to keep your love boat skimming briskly into the future.

The Bottom Line: You're the perfect foil for one another and can make this last for years. **Rating: *******

What Does the Future Hold?

Until 2012, Saturn urges you to be very careful with your investments, insurance, and cash. Be hands-on with financial advisers, instead of assuming that they're so good-hearted that they take a personal interest in your individual account. Be a noisy, squeaky wheel that questions every change, statement, tax change, and market rise or fall. Make sure your financial adviser knows that you will not be ignored or mishandled.

Neptune continues to create romance part of the time, and confusion the rest of the time, in all partnerships, romantic and personal, until 2012. After that, relationships actually start to make more sense and flow more smoothly. You've got loads to look forward to, Ms. Virgo.

How to Interact with a Virgo

DO:

- Pay attention to hygiene. Virgo is a stickler for a bug-free, germ-free environment.
- Arrive on time even if Virgo doesn't. It'll earn you bonus points in the long run.
- Get all the details about a trip, job, event, or investment before asking Virgo to participate. You'll come off like a chump if you don't.

- Respect Virgo's dietary idiosyncrasies. Somewhere between the dark chocolate, martinis, and coffee is the semblance of a healthy lifestyle.
- Feed Virgo's rather tenuous self-confidence. Comment on what's good and right about Virgo, instead of pointing out weaknesses.

DON'T:

- Find fault and nitpick. Virgo knows a lot more about you than you do about her. If you open the door to faultfinding, you're playing with fire.
- Encourage perfection. Virgo is already obsessed with producing a perfect result and doesn't need any nagging from you.
- Feed Virgo's fear or tendency to worry. Instead, downplay negativity and drama. Change the subject when things get morbid.
- Eat from Virgo's plate without permission. You might as well share a toothbrush.
- Take Virgo for granted. Thank your Virgo for every effort and good deed. Never pass up a chance to remark how irreplaceable Virgo is.

♍

Libra

SEPTEMBER 23–OCTOBER 23

♎

You, You, You

So many phrases are tossed around about your personality: *indecisive, needy, in love with love, vain, fashion victim, afraid of controversy.* These are a lazy person's way of diminishing you into a harmless little lump of Play-Doh that can be controlled, shaped, and smashed into smithereens. While others pigeonhole you as an empty phantasm, you quietly, strategically outpace colleagues, friends, relatives, and, of course, the competition. Because others downplay your ability to make a decision and underestimate your ambition, imagine their surprise when your activities become a cause célèbre that dwarfs just about everything they've ever done. Like it or not, being underestimated does have its moments of joy and satisfaction.

You're far stronger and more resilient and decisive than others suspect. (*Big secret:* You're also a shape-shifter who can be anyone's favorite fantasy or most formidable monster. That's power, baby.) To the gossiping ignoramuses' great disadvantage, they don't bother making the time to notice your rapidly developing skills. You can blend in with a bunch of bikers, then freshen up and easily mingle with the glitterati A-list. Versatility (a signature trait of Air signs—Gemini, Libra, Aquarius) gives you remarkable survival skills, no matter what shape the world, economy, or environment is in.

Your key survival tactic is to bend, blend, and assimilate so effectively that others hardly notice. You've perfected this talent to the point that it's become one of your favorite launching pads for corporate and social success. Your easygoing manner, attractive, seemingly accessible exterior, and willingness to cooperate disarm nearly every person you meet. They drop their guard just long enough for you to swiftly, discreetly slip into their shoes and walk away with the top job—and maybe even the most desirable man. Most people never see it coming, because you're so clever and light on your feet.

You've perfected a shrewd talent of not drawing attention to yourself while you're performing covert research—maybe on a man who is borderline committed to another or maybe on a fantastic, rolling-in-riches job. You understate your passion, ambition, and intention to walk away with the spoils, so most people are too self-absorbed to view you as a threat.

Libra falls under the categories of the Air elements and the cardinal signs. Air element signs (Gemini, Libra, Aquarius) are thought to be versatile, intellectually curious, fey, clever, and often insatiable when it comes to attention, parties, white lies, and flirtation. Cardinal signs (Aries, Cancer, Libra, Capricorn) are the pragmatic action figures—the ones that say, "Cut to the chase and draw up the contract, you lazy s.o.b.!" Like all cardinal signs, you cut your fangs on action, ambition, and accomplishment. It's all about the walk and not the talk.

If you were born in the first ten days of Libra, you're the quintessential Libra, kind of girly yet possessing a keen mind for law, human rights, ethics, and responsibility. If you were born in the second ten-day decanate, you're a Libra with Aquarian tendencies, making you an eccentric, ingenious, stubborn, ahead-of-your-time iconoclast. You enjoy shocking and surprising others with expletives spoken so fast that they couldn't be deleted on live TV—and you adore making old ladies blush while listening to your sexual escapades. You might consider science as a career, but erotic books and movies come in a pretty close second. If you're born in the last ten days of Libra you fall into the spectacular Gemini decanate, making you the cleverest, wickedest, most seductive minx in the Libra family. You're the most fun and hardest to pin down.

Anyone thick enough to underestimate the sheer femme fatale potency of Libra doesn't qualify to live in your divine and beautiful universe.

Stars with your star sign: Kate Winslet, Parminder Nagra, Naomi Watts, Ashlee Simpson, Hilary Duff, Donna Karan, Gwyneth Paltrow, Mira Sorvino, Janeane Garofalo, Catherine Zeta-Jones, Susan Sarandon, and Sarah Ferguson.

If You Were an Animal . . .

You'd be an amazing, intelligent cuttlefish that can transform, change color, and instantly blend into your environment—and then quickly disappear into your surroundings when under attack. You thrill and constantly surprise others with a seemingly endless range of characteristics that make you one of the most fascinating, versatile creatures on earth.

Career and Money

The biggest question is, what *can't* you do? A quick study, and even quicker to find a specialty, instantly ups your perceived value in the big boys' eyes. You are not above utilizing every God-given bit of beauty, vocal talent, intelligence, style, and grace to get what you want. You're Venus-on-the-half-shell beautiful, and people often equate beauty with innocence or good behavior. Imagine their surprise when they discover what a ferocious wolf you are in cuddly lamb's clothing, likely to munch your competitors with great gusto for lunch.

So whether you're auditioning for a cameo role on a TV series or running for political office, you always stand out, distinguishing yourself from other contenders who lack your luminous skin, glowing, healthy hair, and winning smile. Icing on the cake: Very few are as tantalizing, charming, wickedly smart, and hilariously funny as you are when you're feeling devilish. You intuitively understand the importance of a good visual impression. You also understand that a well-modulated voice, coupled with faultless preparation, can win you a plum role or career coup. Always look your best. And always do detailed research on the business or person you're meeting with. Your interest alone will make you a standout.

You gain strength from the bonds and alliances you form, both personally and professionally. Your ascent is measured by societal observations of others' success, as well as lessons culled from experience. You also rise to the top because you use your professionalism and the priceless inside info you receive from confidants.

You and your select, loyal cabal of advisers, image tenders, and unconditionally protective friends carefully craft your image. You deftly scamper up the success ladder (oozing charm and blowing air kisses all the way) and receive high marks that blow away your competitors. This is not to say that you don't work hard—you do!—but you're also very lucky, particularly when it comes to your superior gene pool. Even when you make a gargantuan mistake, others view it as a good start or a brave effort. This gift can backfire when you forget that the laws of nature apply equally to you—i.e., breaking promises, being untrustworthy, acting snotty or entitled, and frequent tardiness don't bode well for a brilliant career, so keep a copy of that rulebook nearby.

There's something about you that makes others want to shelter you, take the blame for your mistakes, and absolve you of any wrongdoing or bad decisions. No matter how high and mighty you become, you still radiate a kind of sweetness that others hunger for, relate to, and want to take home and love forever.

Health

If you're one of those typical Libras who battle headaches; persistent painful bladder infections, sometimes followed by kidney infections; low back pain; and a generally hormone-induced case of the blues, you're normal. If bladder infections are very frequent, or they include blood, high blood pressure, or fever, go to your doctor. Drink plenty of water, and parsley tea, and eat enough asparagus to choke a horse.

If you have a family history of cystitis, kidney ailments, or hypertension, get regular medical checkups—and please don't use smoking as a weight control crutch. Smoking is hellish on your bladder and ruins your famous peachy, smooth skin.

Friends and Family

You meet lots of people because you're a very social person. You're also curious about the world, who's dating whom, and what famous artist, architect, or writer is visiting your town. You enjoy meeting new people and learning more about what they do and the world they live in. Most of you are skillful at drawing information out of others without giving away very much about your own life. Each encounter with someone new, no matter how brief, becomes an exciting learning experience—one to share with your friends and family.

Your family members view you as a smart, educated, adventurous star. They love your stories and enjoy listening to you tell about your humorous, sometimes unbelievable encounters with important people. You stand out in your close group of lifetime pals and favorite family members—and appear glamorous and uptown to them.

No matter how successful you become, you still need the balance, comfort, and loyalty of friends and family. They are your roots. You need to earn and keep their love, respect, and loyalty. If you forget a birthday or anniversary, or say you're too busy to attend your family's holiday dinner, feelings will be hurt. No matter how busy, tired, or distracted you are, it's essential to remain in active contact with the people who made you what you are today. Cherish your old friends and family members. Make them a top priority.

Love

When you fall in love, don't hypnotize yourself into believing that you can change the man you plan to live with, marry, or date exclusively. What you see is what you get. Accept or reject it and leave the Cinderella fairy tale on your childhood bookshelf.

Another thing: Stop arguing or shutting down his views because he doesn't agree with you. You can learn a lot from listening to disparate views Even if you remain on opposite sides in a debate, you can agree to disagree instead of ravaging and savaging each opposing idea with explosive innuendo. Life is too short for needless meanness.

Libra + Aries

This is an exciting, yet oddly balanced blend. Aries pokes you with little barbs that sometimes rub you the wrong way and other times excite you into a Kama Sutra state of mind. You kind of dig Aries' bad-boy impulsivity. It makes you feel alive and allows you to live outside of your usual good-girl (read: repressed) standards. Let that bra strap slide down your shoulder; wear a skirt that shows off your noteworthy haunches. Once you've got your horny, high-energy, competitive Ram hooked on your essence de lust, that booty call turns him on and makes him drool, kiss, lick, and squeeze his pillow in his dreams. But when things get serious, he'll ask you to tone down your party mama look—you know, to impress his mom and all that. He's the kind of bad boy that defends his woman's honor and won't listen to anyone talking smack about you, his *principessa*. And he sure as hell needs Mom's approval of his number one girl.

The Bottom Line: Love that begins hotter than a pyroclastic flow, this can gradually settle into a deep, solid, abiding romance that surges on forever and ever. Good from start to finish. **Rating: *******

Libra + Taurus

If you're in the mood to test your patience, and to experience new heights in exotic sexual experiences, this bud's for you. You're more talkative than he is and may find him slightly less effervescent than your bubbly, social, "Hi! I'm single! Yippee!" personality. Some of you initially find him boring. But that can change after the first skin-to-skin encounter. It starts with his eyes: They captivate you, pull you in, wrap you in soft cashmere warmth, and hold you oh so close. You're flattered and surprised by his possessiveness. You feel like you're his woman, his dream girl, his most treasured fantasy—or should we say *possession*? And the passion that pulls you close together is so hot and incredible that you can't find the word "no" in your vocabulary. You will be expected to make concessions. He is possessive and jealous, and at times will treat you like his personal property. It won't be easy: There will be battles for control—who's right, who's wrong, *who's lying*? His rules rule, FYI. You are expected to listen and hold your tongue. But in the best-case scenario, this can be a highly charged, old-world love story.

The Bottom Line: If you're willing to surrender to this man and forgive his monogamy lapses, this could be a life-changing, life-enhancing bond. A challenge worth accepting if you're equal parts tough and docile. **Rating: *****

Libra + Gemini

You two are almost too clever to behave like normal people. You love to play pranks on hapless relatives who never actually get the joke. You two get along so well, never stop yapping, and could host the perfect radio or TV talk show. Who cares that you don't share the same political and social views? You're both willing to say or do anything for a laugh and fabulous ratings. Somewhere in your DNA is the genome for show business. When you two get together, it's always showtime, baby! Your Achilles' heel is that you both want to be the center of attention—not just sometimes, *all the time*. Since competition is inevitable and one-upmanship is an hourly pastime, you need to learn to keep it fun, friendly, and good-hearted. If you can manage that, you've got the makings of a lifelong comedy skit that entertains not only you, but also your friends, kids, and neighbors. You're the kind of couple that volunteers to keep a friend's parrot while he travels through the Scottish Highlands for a month. By the time your friend returns to pick up his bird, the bird's language skills will include fabulous obscenities (probably in French or Italian, of course). You sure have a way with animals.

The Bottom Line: Really fun and packed with friends, travel, and joie de vivre. No matter where you go, you're the life of the party and never waste time being dour, boring, or too serious. If you pass this one up, check your pulse.
Rating: *****

Libra + Cancer

Let's face it, a timid, asexual, antisocial Crab that couldn't match a jacket with a pair of slacks isn't the kind of man you want to be seen with. There's nothing wrong, at least in your book, with being vain. In fact, vanity attracts vanity, so you get exactly what you deserve. Traditionally, this pairing has scratches and scabs on it from numerous catfights and bitch sessions, but if you genuinely love each other and aren't just using each other for career or financial advantage, it can sparkle like a three-carat Cartier diamond.

The Bottom Line: Often this devolves into a marriage or connection of convenience—heavy on glitz but a bit light on substance. **Rating: ****

Libra + Leo

You're good together. You even look perfectly matched, gloriously coiffed, and deliciously in love. Yes, the two of you live for love, not a germ-free clean kitchen that meets military inspection. You live for silk sheets wrapped around your damp, tangled arms and legs. You can be controlling of each other at times—mostly because your world revolves around each other. No one matters more than the object of your intense obsession. You love to read your favorite books to each other, by Anaïs Nin and Henry Miller. And don't forget the Song of Solomon. And there are always your special movie nights, in bed, watching the heart-stopping, endless, enduring love in *Atonement*.

The Bottom Line: Are you kidding? If you can't figure this out, test your hormone levels. Global warming started when you two got together. **Rating:** *****

Libra + Virgo

You like and respect Virgo. Not only does he have a better credit rating than you do (hence your fervent push to get an apartment together), he's also gainfully employed while you're, well, not. But in your defense, you're looking for work every other day. You admire a lot about Virgo—his financial fitness, influential friends, work ethic—and is he ever one sharp dresser! You have to borrow his credit card so that you can buy clothes that at least harmonize with his elite image. You don't like looking like a charity case. Virgo keeps you guessing, feeling slightly paranoid, and always on guard, mostly because you need him more than he needs you. This delicious Virgo man, however, symbolizes an easier lifestyle, complete with diamonds, a maid, a Bentley, and that whole filthy rich fantasy. But if you don't trust him when he leaves on those long business trips that you're not invited to attend, how secure are you? Again, if you're chasing the gravy train instead of the love train, you'll most likely get old and tired, making it easy for him to take notice of plenty of younger, prettier, successful women that are his equal in every category. Make yourself into someone desirable, capable, passionately successful—and not just available to this guy. Take care of yourself and your credit rating. Then start shopping around.

The Bottom Line: Doubtful at best. Painful and humiliating at worst. **Rating: ***

Libra + Libra

You can do well together. You're both lovers of beauty, romance, art, fine wine, European ski resorts, and Parisian and Venetian food. You love most of the same things. But as sensual and quality conscious as you are, you may not have a very high heat factor keeping your romance in tip-top condition. One or both of you may stray. One or both of you may experiment with same-sex alliances and decide that, yes, you're gay. You're so alike that you sense each other's thoughts, plans, secrets, and need for so much more than you can offer each other. Yes, you do provide a nice lifestyle for each other—but where is the deep Charlotte Brontë craving for love? It's MIA, sad to say. Are there ways to light the flame? Well, of course there are. But it's a constant, ongoing effort. If you have children together, they become the center of your universe. You may stay together for the children and the lifestyle, but you always feel incomplete. Think long and hard before going down this road. Once you're on it, it could be a dead end.

The Bottom Line: You've met your doppelgänger—a true vanity connection. Now what? There are so many more interesting options. Why settle? **Rating: ***

Libra + Scorpio

Dear Libra Goddess, this is heat personified! You have met your match and then some. You cannot manipulate, fool, cajole, or confuse Scorpio. He's got you all figured out and under his large, bulbous, lucky thumb before you can say "yes, master." As independent as you can be, you also enjoy those moments of being told when to stand up, sit down, strip off your panties, and walk slowly back in forth in front of him. The only catch here is that you might be Scorpio's little trick on the side. He might have a wife, kids, a busy social life, and a couple other girls for entertainment purposes that you're not aware of. One thing you've got to learn about Scorpio: If you reveal a secret of his, no matter how insignificant it seems to you, you are banished forever. There are no exceptions. And don't think for a moment that he's going to sacrifice his plush life, great wife, and adorable kids for your bedroom skills. It won't happen. Plenty of Scorpio men have stretched out that "separation" or "divorce" ruse for years. Meanwhile, your hair turns gray. Anyway, if he's actually available, you need to keep up with him mentally. Because you're smart, you'll manage just fine. You've also got to have a quick, biting sense of humor and be able to surprise him, sometimes to the point of almost scaring him. He loves a challenge. He wants someone more exotic, quixotic, and talented. If you're up for this challenge, you'll be one satisfied, passionately in love woman. All your jealous girlfriends will hate you.

The Bottom Line: Be the best you can be. This prize

is worth winning and can last a very rewarding lifetime—as long as he's available. **Rating: ****

Libra + Sagittarius

With your combined intellectual curiosity, there's a lot to talk about. You make great friends and share common interests. Politically, you may share the same beliefs. The two of you tend to attract plenty of friends. You might find Sagittarius is more of a loner than you are. Alone time isn't your favorite thing. Sagittarius loves those breathers away from crowds—scaling mountains, writing his novel, or working in his studio. You, a famous multitasking maven, enjoy talking on the phone while throwing together a dinner salad and chatting up pals standing by you in the kitchen. This sort of thing drives a Sagittarius off the nearest cliff. Give your Sagittarius his space. Despite all the clichés about Sagittarians being blarney-blathering bombasts, it's not true. Sagittarius loves his own thoughts, privacy, nature, study, and spiritual communion. After all those good things have been procured, Sagittarius feels justified in spending too much money or in downing an entire bottle of Jack Daniel's. That's called balance in Sagittarius-speak. So it's your call. It may not be a dream sequence for you, but it might suffice as a decent love affair.

The Bottom Line: Iffy. Might fly, might not. If you have your own hobbies, passions, and friends, this stands a chance of lasting. Your alliance generally begins well, but, like a Potemkin village, eventually falls apart. **Rating: ****

Libra + Capricorn

Not an easy blend but a very solid, secure connection. If you're insecure, needy, and require constant reminders that you're smart, scintillating, and the most gorgeous woman in the room, a Capricorn might let you down. What you can expect is tangible proof of his intentions: a marriage proposal, a rock that would make Mariah Carey envious, and a house that might make Donald Trump bite his knuckles. Capricorns don't talk love—they live it. They demonstrate their affection and adoration and rarely forget an anniversary. They protect you and are willing to defend you to the death, if necessary. They worry about your safety, security, and comfort. They spoil the living daylights out of you. This relationship works best if you're mature for your age and can easily move from one level of society to another with aplomb. It also helps if you're discreet and believe in charitable causes. If this doesn't sound good to you, see a shrink.

The Bottom Line: You have just found Mr. Goodbar—only this time it has a happy ending. This connection gets even better over time. **Rating: ******

Libra + Aquarius

This should work famously for both of you. You're both secret rebels and love to think that you invented the next big trend that will transform the art, fashion, or political world. And you both have a love/hate relationship with law, conformity, community standards, and any intrusion into your private life and personal freedom. You may not have a conventional relationship. Most likely, it's open. You both know that it's open but may not discuss it or allow others in on your secret. You may enjoy taking separate vacations—call them business trips, if you like. The point is that you both need a little time apart to absorb new ideas, cultures, people, and worldly awareness. Aquarius may pursue spiritual or religious beliefs or lifestyle choices that are slightly different from your preferences. This doesn't have to keep you apart, but it may generate some tension over time. At times, you find Aquarius just a little too weird for your tastes. At other times, you adore his zany, extraterrestrial sense of humor.

The Bottom Line: This has the bones of an excellent relationship, but will require work. Definitely worth the ups, downs, and pratfalls. **Rating: *****

Libra + Pisces

Tricky but possible. First of all, you probably work or live in pretty close proximity to each other. (Makes secret sneaky kisses and cuddling even more exciting!) You also really dig the way Pisces likes to make you out to be the most beautiful creature he's ever laid eyes on. (Who cares if it's true? It feels so damned good!) Look, you're both hopeless romantics with permanent stars in your eyes and a keen desire for gifts, vacations, and, well, becoming a star, baby. You share movie dates and love to imagine what riding in a white Rolls-Royce might feel like, or maybe even hitching a ride on a private, plush jet. As glam and fun as this can be, here's the fatal catch: Pisces expects to be taken care of and bitterly resents being taken advantage of. So if you have to stay late at a meeting and Pisces is waiting at home, anticipating a night of dirty love, you, Ms. Libra, may end up sleeping in the doghouse.

The Bottom Line: Don't expect Pisces to support you unless he comes with a generous trust fund. He figures his sexual finesse is worth at least a grand a week. You are so much smarter than this. **Rating: ****

What Does the Future Hold?

In late 2009, Saturn pushes into Libra. This is the epitome of growing up, especially if you're in your late twenties, experiencing your first Saturn Return. (The Saturn Return marks the moment in anyone's life when Saturn returns to the spot where it was when that person was born, and it is followed by two and a half to three years of big, grown-up decisions.) Even if you're in your teens or your thirties, forties, and beyond, you feel Saturn's influence. Pay attention to habits or thoughts that lead to addictions, divorce, and so on. You stop being impulsive and consider the consequences of thoughts, words, and deeds. You start to recognize the connection between your behavior, other people's quality of life, and the environment (one lit cigarette carelessly tossed can do unfathomable damage). In other words, you become more conscious and conscientious. This is a total inside job. Others can prompt you to make changes, but you are the one who makes that decision.

How to Interact with a Libra

DO:

- Compliment her sense of style, hair, complexion, and weight loss (real or imagined).
- Learn to get along with her friends and be more sociable.
- Say yes to all festive birthday parties.
- Keep secrets and cover for her when she's been a bad girl (Libras are forever grateful to their enablers).
- Offer to attend exercise class and meet with some miraculous weight control guru with her—moral support and all that.
- Learn to love her tiny, yappy, shedding, allergy-producing little mutt. That dog is precious to her—maybe more precious than you.
- Treat her family members with respect, and never reveal what you and she are up to in front of her mom and dad. View this as an *omertà*.
- Go shopping together—and be honest. If the jeans she's squeezing into make her caboose look wider than Texas, find a nice way to steer her toward something more flattering.

DON'T:

- Nitpick her appearance. This hurts, never helps. Offer solutions, not insults.
- Find fault with her friends or spread gossip from one friend to another. Word gets around fast, and you'll get banned from the group so fast your hemorrhoids will act up.
- Flirt with her boyfriend—not under any circumstances. Getting too friendly with him will earn you a fresh cow-patty facial. This is nonnegotiable.
- Horn in on any positions, titles, or opportunities she's competing for. If you do, you will make a fierce, unforgiving enemy.

Scorpio

♏

You, You, You

Pegged by naïfs as the debauched, depraved Marquis de Sade of the zodiac, you have remarkably high standards; a complex, detailed code of ethics; and an endless fascination with the cycle of life and death.

Emotions boil while you present a "leave me alone—*I'm fine*" exterior. You never forget a former friend's disloyalty, an idol's fall from grace because of dishonesty or cowardice, or another's lack of appreciation of the generous things you've done. *You keep score.* Yes, you have principles that sometimes transform you into a hermit living in a controlled environment; i.e., dominated by rules, high standards, and an almost obsessive fascination with more heroic, more romantic eras—say, the twelfth century. You feel that you were born too late or too soon (mostly too late). Even when you have a companion, you harbor deep secrets that are never fully explained. Many of you choose animal companions over humans because you know they won't betray and are more inclined to obey.

Sexual innuendos and back-stabbing gossip about you being some sort of power-grabbing control freak start early, like as soon as you're strapped into your car seat, and continue relentlessly throughout life. Despite your earnestness, loyalty, and staunch efforts to bail out sloppy friends after their numerous DUI arrests, you still get the rep of perverse sexual athlete with a calculating heart of stone. So not true. The truth is that you have remarkable willpower in certain areas. Without it, you might be as mediocre as most of the uninspired dweebs surrounding you. But with your formidable willpower, you overcome incredible odds, such as surviving an abusive or addictive home life or some other shocking family tragedy. Many of you fully recover (and then some) and become the first person in your family to get a real education (that *you* paid for, of course) or become a sports or entertainment superstar against all odds. You're allergic to failure and refuse to be average. Actually, being average *is* failure as far as you're concerned. Your intense desire to overcome odds and compete goes a long way in determining how far up the success ladder you'll go. Settling for average isn't part of your internal wiring. Astrologically speaking, your life is a microcosm of birth, death, and rebirth. You live this cycle every day, learning tough lessons and either growing exponentially to zoom up the ladder of success or failing miserably, licking your wounds and going into hiding until you figure out what went wrong. When you fail, you come back hard, tough-minded, and victorious. You learn your lessons and are determined to never repeat particularly nasty ones. You always win, even if it takes several tries. The tougher the challenge, the more gritty and relentless you are. It's rare to be born Scorpio without having considerable challenges and struggles to overcome.

People who underestimate you are slow learners. Patience, always a challenge, is something you cultivate throughout life, like a venomous viper looking for a meal. You don't randomly strike at small targets that aren't desirable and won't fill you. You aim for bigger, more ambitious prizes. You may even bond with your target prior to striking and paralyzing him, and then happily consume every last juicy bit of him. You learn to disguise your anxiety about things not happening quickly enough. Others assume that you're steady as a rock until they discover that you sometimes resort to vodka, antianxiety meds, and sleeping aids just to stay even and not jump out of your skin. You require patience in order to conduct strict quality checks before releasing a masterpiece to an eager crowd of critics and supporters. Like your alter ego, the viper, you're a strategist. None of your "big win" accomplishments ever happens quickly or easily for you. Most of your life-changing victories include years of learning, struggle, revision, and a few humbling flops along the way. Learning curves and struggles aside, you end up on top and get the last laugh. A number of people who are denied access to you interpret your secrecy as coldness. Well, here's the 4-1-1: *It's protective!*

Yours is a Water sign—an emotional holding cell for every sigh, scream, and gentle or rough touch you've ever experienced. Memories stay with you *forever*. This creates a very crowded consciousness. Sometimes, in desperation for relief, escape, and most of all, oblivion, you drink or drug excessively. Water signs tend to tumble quite easily into addiction. You can avoid becoming one of them by not allowing the addictive process to get started in the first place. Yes, the world is often too much for you, complete with loss, heartache, and a deep desire for someone or something just out of reach, but substance abuse doesn't fix the problem.

The first ten days of Scorpio are true-blue, 100 percent Scorpio. If you were born then, you have a direct manner and always seem to be busy. This group is the most authentic of all Scorpios. The next ten days are influenced by Pisces, emphasizing your sensitivity, psychic ability, glamour, and artistic talent. You may also possess very beautiful eyes. The final ten days of Scorpio are influenced by Cancer, giving you a caring, affectionate nature. You're a natural collector, good in business, and possibly a gourmet chef.

Yours is also one of the fixed signs: Taurus, Leo, Scorpio, Aquarius. This makes you stubborn, strong-willed, and a creature of habit. No one can make you do much of anything. You have to want to do it, and you refuse to be harassed or manipulated by a do-gooder friend or relative. Being a powerful fixed Water sign guarantees that you'll get pretty much what you want.

One of your earliest challenges (besides the usual "Am I too fat? Ugly? Weird?") is deciding who you want to be and how you want to make an indelible mark on the world. You learn at an early age that others might not assist you simply because you need help. In many cases, friends may be more supportive and interested in your success and happiness than family members who are battling their own issues. So your survival instincts start early. You develop an incredible radar for detecting others' sincerity, generosity, or intention. You wall yourself off from people who had the chance to be honest with you—but refused to.

Trust is your Holy Grail and Ark of the Covenant. Many of you believe that trust is a form of perfection, impossible to achieve. The more cynical among you believe that trust is for schlubs with a desire to be punished and humiliated. Most of you, however, still believe in trust, and might actually trust someone, at least until he or she screws up. Smart compromise requires a lot of thought, careful analysis, and extra time to get things right. A brilliant compromise can help you make peace with being a single person for the foreseeable future or remaining a married person with a lovable but flawed mate. Those of you who *strategically compromise* are likely to find peace, happiness, and prosperity that can last a lifetime. Even better, there is no sign of desperation tattooed on your forehead.

Stars with your star sign: Demi Moore, Hillary Rodham Clinton, Julia Roberts, Meg Ryan, Sylvia Plath, Maria Shriver, Joni Mitchell, Parker Posey, Whoopi Goldberg, Fran Lebowitz, and Goldie Hawn.

If You Were an Animal . . .

Many people consider you an amazing animal in the sex, mental toughness, and power departments. Your counterpart in the animal world is a sleek, powerful, probably deadly (or at the very least, capable of stunning its prey) viper—a wary loner at heart, but open to a mate that has a good chance of providing protection and satisfaction. Quiet, private, and unafraid of the dark, you have formidable strength but reveal it only when necessary. Idle threats aren't part of your survival repertoire. When you strike, the games stop and serious business begins. Finding your equal may not be possible. Finding someone able to complement and enhance your lifestyle is definitely within your grasp.

Career and Money

You choose role models (rarely, if ever, are they family members) and mimic them. You dutifully, even humbly, play apprentice and absorb all their career, status, and success secrets. People tell you proprietary and shockingly personal things they wouldn't dare reveal to anyone else. The Apt Pupil and Bitch Confessor of the zodiac, you know how to yank info out of others better than anyone. This educational process could go on for an entire summer break or continue for years. You don't separate from your willing source of knowledge, contacts, and potential revenue until you've learned the ropes and have exceeded your teacher's competency level. You *always* have a grand plan—and make a very dangerous personal assistant. *Pourquoi?* Well, mostly because you race to the top of the competitive heap faster than your teacher and are far more willing to do *whatever* is necessary to succeed. Depending on how observant your role model is, he or she probably won't even see your power grab and departure until it's all over. You're always looking up, fascinated by big scores, rags-to-riches stories—and, most of all, redemption in the face of disgrace. This redemption theme repeats itself throughout your very long life.

Career choices require loads of compromise and reality-based goals. And reality-based goals are a lot harder to create than they sound. You pick what seems to be an ideal role model partially because you admire (and want) what he or she has. Your fantasy is to rise higher up the ranks than your role model's airy perch on the fiftieth floor. But is this realistic? If you set the bar too high before you've actually started, could you doom yourself to failure and defeat? Consider diverse interests, jobs, and locations. Don't limit your options—ever. Finding that perfect sweet spot that fulfills all or most of your needs requires time, research (you're gifted at research and spying, when necessary), and effort. A lot of Scorpios are herded into medical, technical, and financial fields by ambitious relatives or bossy mentors. Many of you passionately love your work—herded or not—while some of you make an uneasy peace with a so-so career because of the time and money spent on your education. Settling for "almost right" in a career is a prelude to yet another job hunt. Strategic compromise, a surplus of inside info, and fabulous contacts are your weapons of choice when it comes to achieving your dream career. No one is tough enough to outlast you. You are an impossibly hot act to follow.

Health

Your digestive system, given to rumbling and food allergies, is always an annoying reality. Irritable bowel problems, uterine and fallopian tube issues, and bladder and ovarian uproars may simultaneously occur. These problems can generate horrible premenstrual tension: pain, headaches, backaches, bloating, mood disorders—and worst of all, you feel miserably *fat*. So being the sign most intimately associated with juicy genitalia and a me-so-horny root chakra can be a royal pain in the ass, especially during your periods. Ovulation isn't exactly dancing with the stars, either. Word to expectant moms: When it comes time to decide natural or C-section after a few hours of hard yet unproductive labor, just say C-section and get it over with. And unless your doctor or physical condition suggests otherwise, maintain a clean, low-fat, low-sugar, lean protein, and complex carb diet. Your dramatically reduced cellulite and lean, sleek arms and thighs (not to mention a sudden disappearance of back fat) will thank you profusely. And those heart-stopping sexy size 2 frocks you've lusted for—and can finally shimmy into—will, too. Managing stress isn't for sissies. You do your best to look cool under gut-wrenching pressure, no matter how many pink slips are emptying the increasingly silent workstations surrounding you. There may come a time when you need a therapist to shelter you from a mini tsunami of anxiety. Drum circles, sage burning, and healing stone massages can only go so far. Blend modern and ancient traditions and medicine for a more effective shot at relief. You're one of those busy people who can't afford to stop everything and whine for weeks at a time. When you're anxious or depressed, get help immediately. Hey, Scorpio: You're too important to not be fully functional.

Friends and Family

You're amazingly effective at preventing others from getting too close, largely as a means of self-protection. After being pushed away a half dozen times, those people might get defensive and label you an arrogant, cold snob. There may come a time when you have things just the way you want them, but find yourself feeling alone. You're not afraid of being alone, but still complain about loneliness. (Kvetching is actually one of your specialties, FYI.)

You don't require a mob of friends and acquaintances to feel secure, loved, and significant. You're far too privacy loving for that. You do form very tight connections that tend to last for tens of years with a select group of friends and carefully chosen family members. People who are lucky enough to be handpicked by you understand how extraordinary this honor is. They also know that if they ever betray or take advantage of you, they'll be booted out of your private inner circle. You value quality, not quantity.

Love

People often misunderstand your idealism. You have a vision of an incomparable life, friendship, or love and are unlikely to let go of it. Some of you get involved with a cast of characters who each possess elements of the ideal mate but fall short of the finish line. Even if you tossed them all together, they'd come up short. Each time you settle for less, you feel more convinced that the right guy doesn't exist—a genuine self-fulfilling prophecy. (Hmm . . . maybe it's time to stop settling.) Working toward that dream of a life, love, and calling is *too precious to give up on*. Ask Demi Moore if you have further questions. Ask Hillary Clinton if you're still in doubt. In the interest of common sense, it's important to state that not all compromises are sellout dream killers.

Scorpio + Aries

You're initially attracted to Aries because you adore his honesty, stunning sexual energy (*big* points for that!), and heroic, protective knight-in-shining-armor vibe. It's kind of thrilling to be desired by such an amorous man-beast. The first rush of hotness is so intense that you almost pass out. So it's a real page-turner to begin with, but it becomes a twisted fairy tale when he starts reaching for the harness to control you. *No one controls you.* A man's attempt to do so slams the brakes on your libido, no matter how effective the foreplay. You cannot be lassoed and hog-tied by any-one. Scorpio rejects being shouted at or ordered about. So this little adventure starts off hot, hot, hot, but after several confrontations over jealousy and who gets to be boss, the heat turns cold, cold, cold.

The Bottom Line: You're more sophisticated, smart, and sexually experienced than he'll ever be. This blend gets points for a rollicking, overheated start. Tragically, it fades in the stretch. Not exactly an eternal flame. **Rating: ****

Scorpio + Taurus

You get along so well, despite being two ultrastubborn people. This lusciously close attachment begins with intense sexual attraction. Neither of you is willing to give in during a heated debate or (shudder) admit to wrongdoing. You're like two opposing attorneys with gargantuan determination to win. Well, actually, the point is to humble and bring your opponent to his knees—no matter how long or exhausting the battle. On the other hand, you actually need each other for balance and growth—and of course, great sex that feels so good that you're unwilling to go without it. One look at Taurus's food issues helps you finally understand your own food foibles. You forgive him his weight trespasses, especially when he gives you a sexy, sensual massage, followed by dirty love. Sex is magic for both of you. And the fact that he's so stunningly well-endowed doesn't hurt a bit. Don't allow petty spats and stubbornness to interfere with your life-changing, hot, psycho-sexual-spiritual connection. This one has "forever" and "great sex" painted all over it.

The Bottom Line: Sexy, luscious, edible Taurus is a candy store, ready for you to gobble and enjoy. This one's a keeper. Instead of blaming him for being stubborn, curb your own stubborn streak. Just get the loyalty and monogamy thing worked out on day one and you've got it made. **Rating: *******

Scorpio + Gemini

You uncover a whirling blizzard of non sequiturs, highly charged sexual excitement, and endless entertainment in Gemini. It's impossible to be bored. Gemini lures you to experiment with new sexual techniques (*oh, goody!*) that open you up emotionally. Your quicksilver Gemini defies aging and gravity and scoffs at logic. Some of your most pronounced growth and success (not to mention self-awareness) come from Gemini's urging you to move away from tedious habits, deeply ingrained family guilt, and traumatizing traditions. This connection won't be easy. It requires work and commitment from each of you. But you can build a great life full of sexy spontaneity you would've missed without a wild-ass Gem by your side. The two of you are so much more than the sum of your delectable and impressive parts. In fact, when you get together and remain together, you push each other up several notches socially and financially, becoming a bona fide power couple.

The Bottom Line: This coupling is fueled by transformation. You have to work hard to keep this one in top shape, but the payoff is worth every ounce of effort. If you have the stamina to remain in this relationship, you'll be much happier and better off in the long and short run. **Rating: ******

Scorpio + Cancer

Other than patches of moody pouting, this pairing earns mostly positive points. You and Cancer are both Water signs, totally in love with privacy, safety, and *control*. You each have well-established boundaries that only an insensitive slob would breach. You share a love of music, fine wine, collectibles, sex, pharmaceuticals, and movies (and you occasionally star in, direct, and film your own sexy movies). You share a private world and guard it *ferociously*. Honor and unconditional trust are required. One betrayal may be more than either of you can accept—so keep your pants on when you're away from each other. Many of you share a love of very specialized, comfortable travel. You enjoy architecture (ancient and modern), museum hopping, and fabulous cuisine.

The Bottom Line: Together you build a private, exclusive club with two dedicated, contented members. This one has great legs, especially if both of you are able to resist the ravages of too much of the good life. **Rating: ******

Scorpio + Leo

Leo excites you and turns you all the way on. From the outside, Leo looks like an exclusive high-end package specially customized for your intense needs. Ironically, needs are also the fly in the ointment. Leo may decide that your need for privacy is a huge snore. Leo also believes that you don't appreciate his entitlements: leisure time, expensive toys, exotic friends you may never be introduced to, and his ex-girlfriends that text, call, and e-mail him incessantly. As a result, Leo feels so unappreciated that he is forced to drag his sorrow and sexual frustration (and erectile dysfunction meds) into other women's beds when he should be gettin' to busy in yours. You may never quite measure up in the attentiveness department as far as Leo is concerned. Warning: Leo can be passive-aggressive and bitchy when he feels neglected—i.e., dropping damaging hints that reveal some of your secrets, career trauma, or digestive issues to friends and colleagues. *Traitor!* Despite all the endless drama, some of you courageously soldier on, excusing his monogamy lapses, thinning hairline, and eventual paunch. No matter how caring and loyal you are, you may be a bitter disappointment for Leo—and he for you.

The Bottom Line: Your best is more than enough for most people, but nothing can measure up to Leo's great expectations. Some connections are better forgotten after the first date. This is one of them. **Rating: ***

Scorpio + Virgo

Some things are meant to be. When you first encounter caring, attentive, thoughtful Virgo, that's precisely what you think. You quickly shut down your surging tide of emotion in an effort to calm down, catch your breath, and regain total control. But OMG, Virgo—his smile, those eyes, that body—always gets the lead role in your most intense, graphic sexual fantasies and quickly becomes your favorite obsession. You love his mind and thoughtfulness—and his attention to detail is second to none. This is the kind of man you could parade in front of your most discerning, impossible-to-please friends and receive a standing ovation. You both have similar goals and standards and a gift for taking oaths and secrets very seriously. You sense that—*damn!*—you might be able to trust him. And should the situation arise when you need transportation, help with an event, or just a really discreet confidant, Virgo is there, ready and willing to serve and pleasure you—and cook your favorite dinner afterward. What more can you ask for? He's usually gifted in bed, a healthy hygiene freak, and aware of everything you do. Your obsession with each other is absolutely wonderful.

The Bottom Line: Friendship, shared interests, wry

humor, loyalty, and earthy sensuality make this one a keeper. You're *so proud* of each other and feel stronger when you're together. A lifelong romance that seems almost too good to be true, but it's *real,* baby. **Rating: *******

Scorpio + Libra

"I know more than you do" conversations become classic, chronic one-upmanship on a daily basis. Biting sarcasm creeps into at least half of your chats. Both of you are smart (you're smarter) and know what to say to get the desired reaction. You suspect that Libra isn't being completely honest with you, has a hidden agenda, and might be seeing someone else. You could be right on all counts. Libra is perfect for a rebound affair. You know that it won't last and are mostly fine with it. He's not your great passion, and you're not his, either. You can look past Libra's little deceptions (and less-than-impressive package) because you don't take Libra all that seriously. Libra can be an excellent port in the storm when you're between jobs, marriages, or hormonal rages. In other words, he'll do in a pinch. Libra is your fallback feel-good solution for about fifteen minutes. And when you're done, toss him back for someone else to use, and everybody wins.

The Bottom Line: Totally temporary, and semiserviceable in a working relationship—even though you never actually trust each other. Not meant to last, but a pretty good pastime until something better comes along. And it always does. Yawn. *Next.* **Rating: ****

Scorpio + Scorpio

You're both extremely competent and accountable, and you have big ideas and even bigger desires. With all the extremes and fireworks, can this relationship work? You bet it can—and how. Once you've experienced this kind of mega-depth, most other relationships seem dull. Sure, you're both jealous, suspicious, more easily hurt than you want anyone to know—and emotional. Topping it off, neither of you ever forgets a slight. But when this works—and it does more often than not—it can turn water into wine. You understand each other's power, strength, secrets, and boundaries—no detailed explanation is necessary. You know what your partner wants and needs and do your best to please. Here's a secret: Female Scorpios generally have more intense, longer-lasting (often multiple) orgasms than male Scorpios. Female Scorpios may be more sexually active and adventurous than male Scorpios. So be prepared to initiate sex in this rich, loving, intensely private alliance. Savor this one: It could last for years.

The Bottom Line: If you love and respect yourself, you find it easy to love and respect another Scorpio. There's no reason to test boundaries in this relationship. It's a deeply romantic, passionate bond that usually produces children and great happiness. **Rating: ******

Scorpio + Sagittarius

Shock, amusement, and entertainment keep you on edge for the next surprise or stunt your Sagittarius tosses at you.

Sagittarians are profligate givers, spenders, and lovers. They can't be contained, controlled, or reined in. It's pointless even to try. You question his judgment, his honesty, and his gambling, drinking, and all-night parties with "friends." Depending on your tolerance for feeling like an overused chump, you might end this thing after the first infraction. You're too careful and protective to put yourself at risk (infections, accidents, debt, heartache) with a Sagittarian. Sagittarius men take a very long time to mature. Along the way, they develop almost savantlike talent and are heralded as guitar gods or athletic wunderkinder. Your Sagittarius is probably great in the sack, too—when he's not hung over or exhausted from a three-way with his unnamed friends. Because certain health and safety issues may emerge during your trial by fire with an exciting but slightly careless Sagittarius, you might end this in a flood of angry tears and become celibate just to punish yourself for falling for him in the first place. Sure, he may have a beautiful mind, but that doesn't make up for his angry primate behavior.

The Bottom Line: Don't put yourself in jeopardy for love, lust, or excitement. Sagittarius creates extreme highs and lows. Unless you're a dedicated codependent, you don't need to make your life revolve around his mania. **Rating:** *

Scorpio + Capricorn

Now here's a blend you can take to the bank—literally. Once the two of you put your genius for marketing, promotion, and finance together, nothing can stop you. But why settle for a huge stash of cash? You also find what feels pretty close to a soul mate in Capricorn—a stellar secret keeper and privacy lover, just like you. And the lust factor is sensational. It's difficult to find a better all-around match when it comes to business, pleasure, or a divine blend of both. You and your Cappie may even resemble each other. You share the same vision of the future and deep craving for redemption. And you both learned early on in life that there's no such thing as a free ride. This one includes excellent communication. You read each other's body language. Even your breathing patterns are similar. Family backgrounds, shared desires, and fear of failure compelled both of you to grow up fast and work hard to be more than others thought possible.

The Bottom Line: You two speak in code to each other. No one can enter your private world without your invitation. Actually, the two of you don't need or want anyone else. **Rating: *******

Scorpio + Aquarius

This blend is all about possibilities and projections. You can mentally transform an Aquarius into your vision of an ideal mate, but it will take a lot of time and concentration. For starters, Aquarius actually does exist in a separate universe. The things that feel so crucial and moving to you are mere blips on a radar screen to him. You're both brainy and given to obsessive conspiracy theory books and movies, but beyond that—where's the beef? You dig and dig for some kernel of deep passion or longing, but seem to find only empty pockets of air. You walk away from Aquarius, wondering what happened—and may never find out what went wrong. You need to understand everything about Mr. Aquarius before hooking up with him, and initially you are attracted to his unique, eccentric, funny oddness. It's a challenge trying to find his hidden vulnerabilities and desire for commitment. Unfortunately, you may never find these very human qualities in Aquarius. It's kind of like falling for an extraterrestrial—exciting initially, but disappointing the longer it drags on. So stop digging and assuming that he feels the same feelings you do. He probably doesn't—and may not want to. He's content being alone. You like being alone, too. But you also want some man-woman closeness from time to time. Getting that kind of satisfaction may not be possible with Aquarius.

The Bottom Line: Don't expect Aquarius to change for you. He's just fine with his odd little reality that may or may not include other human beings. You cannot love him into feeling the way you do, and the sexual frustration is just too much. Why not get a toy poodle or pet monkey? Either one will be far more affectionate and understanding. **Rating: ***

Scorpio + Pisces

This is pure fireworks, offering fun, escape, and unbelievable sex. If you're lucky enough to snag a well-adjusted, gainfully employed Pisces, you're a goner. He'll charm the pants off of you and have your heart before you can say "but I'm married/have a boyfriend." Once you lock eyes with a Pisces, everything else disappears. You fall hard and can't do enough for him. Don't spoil him or become his sugar mama. Make sure that he's responsible, accountable, honest, and all the other good grown-up things. If you can see straight through your hormone-glazed eyes and detach just enough to make sure he's worthy, this one is *the* one for you. You both love life, beauty, design, movies, and memories that you can weave into poetry or music. Pisces bolsters your creativity, while you make him feel more important and adored. You're probably stronger in certain areas than he is, but you two are equals when it comes to great passion and total dedication to each other. Think of the most romantic, heartbreaking movie you've ever seen. That's the kind of passion you and Pisces create. Expect to have children together, unless there's a medical reason preventing it.

The Bottom Line: If he meets the basic requirements (gainfully employed, responsible), don't let him out of your sight. He's your love angel, through and through. **Rating:** *****

What Does the Future Hold?

A big Saturn cycle starts in early October 2012, when Saturn moves into your sign. This Saturn phase will continue until late December 2017. Be fastidious about your hair, skin, and teeth during this time. Instead of just dieting for the sake of skinniness, eat foods that are bone healthy. Feed your skin with gentle cleansers and sunblock. Saturn cycles can age you, unless you take smart preventative steps. Since Saturn is associated with foundations of all sorts (bones, weight-bearing walls in buildings, and traditions that may or may not be healthy to maintain) and the outgrowth of those foundations (teeth, hair, skin, the external body), safeguard your basic foundation. See the dentist. Get regular physicals that include a thyroid test and bone density test. You can emerge looking and feeling better (and probably thinner) from a Saturn transit by being vigilant about your health habits.

How to Interact with a Scorpio

DO:

- Keep mum about secrets or private business that Scorpio shares with you.
- Continue to earn her trust by making good on promises and being dependable.
- Make your relationship special and private. Scorpios don't enjoy mob scenes, unless you've prepared them by saying, "My relatives may be dropping by to see us."
- Remember that her private papers are just that: private. Don't sneak a peek at her e-mail messages or eavesdrop on phone conversations.

- Show gratitude and appreciation for her attention, affection, and hard work. There's a lot to admire about Scorpio. Just show your appreciation in private.

DON'T:

- Discuss her family or business concerns with your friends. She needs to trust you. If she thinks you're blabbing about her private issues to your pals, she'll clam up and shut you out.
- Pick at her about weight gain. Harassment doesn't motivate better diet and exercise choices. Encouragement does.
- Flip out or cry in public. She hates public scenes.
- Lie to her—even if it's a "white lie." White lies offend her just as much as other lies. She's very intuitive and will know when you're fibbing.

Sagittarius

You, You, You

A dedicated adventurer, you honestly believed you could fly like Peter Pan when you were a kid. As an adult, you spend a lot of time in airports, catching planes, getting to meetings, and picking up friends. Maybe you're a pilot or flight attendant or part of airport security. Jet fuel and the physics of flight seem to be hardwired into your spirit.

Known for your honesty and offbeat sense of humor, you're everyone's unpredictable little pet. You might say something totally outrageous at a business meeting or family gathering. It's your way of breaking the tension. Most of your close friends realize this and privately feel relief when you make your "inappropriate" remarks.

You've always been rebellious and are likely to remain so throughout your life. Like all Fire signs (Aries, Leo, Sagittarius), you resent others telling you what to do. You hate to be interfered with while you're deep in thought, working out a phrase in a story or song, or thinking about a dream you had. Insensitive types tend to ignore your subtle signals to buzz off. Sensitive types get it and move on. You do need your space.

If you love animals (chances are you do) you're especially fond of large animals (horses, big dogs, large talking birds). You may prefer the company of animals to that of humans much of the time. They calm you, and they are loyal, loving, and undemanding.

Although you're famously sexual, you're very guarded about intimacy, secrets, and giving up whatever control you've cobbled together. Sometimes, being alone is the ultimate power seat, because there's no one there to boss you around.

One reason so many of you choose a quiet private life is because you have difficulty shutting out other people's thoughts, needs, and emotional struggles. You need to practice detachment for your own emotional health. Many of you suffer silently with depression and anxiety, until fate intervenes and calls attention to your problem. These private struggles also tend to isolate you. The more sensitive you are, the more solitary you tend to be. Even people who know you well have no idea of the battles you cope with, sometimes daily. Just remember, Sagittarius: You are made of stars, very strong stuff, and have a divine purpose on this planet. You're a mouthpiece for advance notice from spirit guides. You need to keep your body strong so that you can complete your work on planet earth.

If you were born during the first ten days of Sagittarius, you're in the first decanate, and the most Sagittarius of all.

You job-hop, go to school for extended periods of time (and change majors several times), write, delay commitment until later in life (if ever), and like to keep your options open. Travel is a big part of your life and your dreams. If you were born during the second ten days, you were born in the Aries decanate of Sagittarius, making you impulsive, killer-competitive, aggressive, stubborn, and athletic. You dare others to knock the chip off your shoulder and may unpredictably strike back at others who allegedly have done you wrong. Silence, study, and freedom mean a lot to you. You normally have problems eating and relaxing unless you're alone. Every interruption or request seems to penetrate your fragile emotional ecosystem. You'd probably be happiest living on an offshore island with Wi-Fi and a few dogs. Men and friends are optional—unless you really, really *want* them. The final decanate of Sagittarius is ruled by Leo, giving you a dramatic, humorous, and sociable demeanor. You're the life of the party and ambitious for money, recognition, fame, and fawning admiration. You love others (especially your lover du jour and your children—with fiery, fierce passion). Unlike the first two decanates, you have a difficult time living alone. You enjoy other people too much to isolate, pass up a potential new love, or indulge your senses with music, wine, and the best of the best.

Yours is a mutable Fire sign. This means that you absorb the thoughts and emotions of those around you. You may not call yourself a psychic, but you are, and oftentimes a very reluctant one. If the people nearby are upset and anxious, you absorb it. Pay very close attention to the people you allow to get close. A number of you seem to attract very needy, psychic vampires who drain away your energy. They also come between you and your purpose on the planet: to inspire, teach, and guide others higher and higher.

Stars with your star sign: Scarlett Johansson, Tina Turner, Christina Applegate, Bette Midler, Caroline Kennedy, Daryl Hannah, Britney Spears, Marisa Tomei, Julianne Moore, Tyra Banks, Dame Judi Dench, Kim Basinger, Milla Jovovich, Liv Ullmann, Katie Holmes, and Christina Aguilera.

If You Were an Animal . . .

You'd be a lone, magnificent jungle cat, hunting at night, guarding your turf, and relishing your domain. Your cubs are precious to you, as are your freedom and territory. Sinewy and powerful, you normally don't make the first move. It's more interesting for you to wait and see what another might do. If others respect your space, no harm, no foul. If they trespass, you'll have them for dinner.

Career and Money

Sometimes you're in the mood to tolerate another's arrogance and sometimes you're *not*. This is one of the millions of reasons for you to work offsite—or hire an assistant to take annoying calls for you.

The bombast and hypocrisy in some office settings offends you. You find it difficult to cope with. You may abruptly leave a job that others would sell their souls for, because you've had it literally *up to here* with office politics and phoniness.

You refuse to submit to rules that seem unnecessary or punitive. You will not cower to another's will. Nobody is the boss of you—except you.

Unfortunately, the world wasn't built around your idealism, ethics, or sense of fair play. Because many of you work well into your later years, you must not only learn to cope with various pernicious forms of corporate culture, but you will also notice the ever-galloping age gap problem. This issue could become more apparent during the next several years, due to adjustments in global economic patterns. Retirement (a one-time expectation) may have to be delayed until death. This is actually good news for most of you, because you've always got a new goal to pursue or adventure to explore. You're not afraid of failure but are very afraid of stagnation.

You always do better as a lone wolf: a behind-the-scenes screenwriter, playwright, poet, political/societal blogger, radio talk show host, environmental activist, or novelist. A free-speech proponent, you view the Internet and all forms of instant information as power to the people.

Because you also have lots of natural talent in acting and other forms of entertainment (including singing, dancing, sports, modeling), you might aim your entrepreneurial arrow at creating your own media empire, available online and through other outlets. You don't do this merely to showcase your talents, but to introduce new talent and ideas to your vast online audience. You have a gift for interviewing others. Your own endless curiosity about what someone else thinks, feels, or does feeds the public's need to understand, too.

Like other Fire signs, you adopt an "I'd rather do it *myself*" attitude, and eschew all offers of help and advice. Try not to be so stubborn. Why not settle down and listen to some of the great (and free) advice being offered to you?

You're not giving away your power. In fact, you might be making it easier for someone who feels deeply in debt to you to resolve that debt by helping you. The least you can do is to give him or her the opportunity, and you might learn some valuable information, too.

Saving money for the future may seem difficult due to changing job status, health issues, and economic high and low tides. Saving and investing are necessary to maintain your independence so keep a sharp eye on your money. Learn to fight for it and protect it, like the jungle cat purring within you.

Health

You cannot stand to be limited in any way, so you take illness or injury as a personal affront.

Your body is usually slender, muscular, and athletic

in youth. As you age, you tend to either put on or significantly drop weight, depending on your lifestyle, health, and genetics. More than half of you will have lower back problems that create slight discomfort (mild sciatica) or a chronic (and literal) pain in the ass. Your back problems usually result from injuries (accidents, falls, overuse) rather than heredity. Be kind to your back.

You tend to look exotic and younger than your years, barring a health problem. Many of you have long earlobes, the ancient symbolic indicator of long life. As a rule, Fire signs tend to live better than most—not just in terms of longevity, but also in terms of quality of life. Staying active helps you reduce stress, keeps your muscles and bones strong, and helps you stay connected with your spiritual side. Motion is your Wi-Fi to the spirit world. The more you walk, run, bike, swim, or ski with the sun on your high forehead and sensitive back, the closer you get to profound spiritual connection.

Your bronchial region is very sensitive, making smoking a definite *no*. Being around a smoky or polluted environment is just wrong. Your lungs need all the fresh air they can get, which might cancel out most big, industrialized cities as a home base or vacation destination for you.

You're also a target for allergens, so be aware of environmental or food-related allergies. Food-related allergies may affect your breathing, skin, throat, and of course your sometimes-cranky digestive system.

Speaking of digestion, you need fiber, lots of healthy liquids (more water, less coffee), and tons of physical exercise that doesn't strain your back.

Of all the health problems you're prone to, back issues tend to be the most debilitating and limiting. Wear your seat belt at all times and be aware of your environment. Car accidents, bike accidents, skiing accidents, and slip-and-fall accidents are all *so you*. Show me a Sagittarius (or Aries) and I'll show you someone with some pretty wild scars.

Friends and Family

Your personal life often sounds like a soap opera. The primary complaint you hear from others is "How come you always make time for *x-y-z*, but not for *me*?"

Guilt and manipulation pervaded your childhood and the pattern continues until you escape by moving far away from home. E-mail and mobile phones prevent total escape, but you try to dodge the mommy or daddy guilt bullet by not answering messages, texts, or calls for as long as possible. Eventually, of course, you have to. Ugh. Your strategy for dealing with picky, toxic friends and family is to avoid, avoid, avoid. This is a temporary fix. Most problematic friends and family members will continue to pester you until you either tell them to get lost or work out a compromise. Sure, you'd love to borrow Harry Potter's Cloak of Invisibility, but you can't hide from certain annoying people forever.

Cringeworthy as it is, you need to sit down and draw out some boundary lines. Some people will not respect your boundaries. Those are the ones to drop from your roster of real friends and nonparasitic family members. You know the types: the users, the grossly self-involved, and the psychos who need tons of therapy. Sometimes you have to cut the cord for your own mental health—and never look back. Sometimes you also have to change your phone number and e-mail address.

Your friends, as a rule, provide more support and understanding than most family members. They accept you *as is* instead of trying to remodel your personality and goals, as well as your choices in men.

Love

You love the idea of love, but not the entanglement that often accompanies it. You don't want to feel owned, controlled, or corralled by someone. Feeling trapped makes you feel anxious, insecure, angry, and depressed.

You'd rather be alone than be smothered by a needy control freak or a paranoid snoop who checks your e-mail and correspondence. If love means giving up your freedom, you'd just as soon live without it.

If you're very lucky, you can find a perfect mate: someone who adores you unconditionally and doesn't try to limit you in any way. Sagittarians are notorious for attracting unexpected luck, sometimes on a grand scale, so there's hope for you—lots of it.

Sagittarius + Aries

You can't wait to get your hands on Aries. He's charming, heroic, and strong enough to keep up with you (that's a tall order). He's relatively low maintenance, too, and rarely gets underfoot. You can move freely through your routines, meditation, work, workouts, and errands without a peep of protest from Aries. He's got plenty to focus on and accomplish, too. To make things even more bodacious, his work and interests may often take him out of town, giving you more space, freedom, and luxurious silence. You share mutual Fire sign imperatives: freedom, control, and progress without interruption. You respect each other as friends and lovers. When you have a serious question, he listens and responds with the wisdom of a much older person. You view him as a sage savant. Your friends may or may not fully understand him or the relationship. They'll get over it. This is an excellent blend.

The Bottom Line: Total keeper with all the trimmings: shared needs and values, big love, and huge respect for each other. **Rating:** *****

Sagittarius + Taurus

The thrill is certainly there: Taurus finds you amazing, sexy, and a total mystery. He tags along, trying to keep up with you (probably not possible), and does all the good-boy things to earn your devotion. His biggest fault is being very possessive and *underfoot*. If he could just develop another interest (besides hitting on your girlfriends) to keep him happily engaged, you could have a superb relationship. He's got so many good points—willing to do the yard work and minor home repairs and take care of you when you're sick—but he blows the love vibe to bits and pieces when he gets pouty, needy, or manipulative. You find yourself feeling as if you're trapped in an airless elevator without a prayer of getting out. So much depends on his maturity. Select a man who is all grown up with friends, interests, and a meaning-ful job that keeps him busy. If you make a smart move like that, you've got a winner.

The Bottom Line: If you've chosen a person who respects you, you're in for a luscious time. If either of you has a deficit in the maturity or communication categories, it probably won't get off the ground. **Rating: ****

Sagittarius + Gemini

You two argue a lot but seem to love it. You're actually extremely well suited for each other and tend to blend ener-gies and priorities remarkably well. Just don't put up with any snotty stuff from Mr. Gemini, who tends to be a bit of a know-it-all. True enough, he's brilliant and adorable, and always has a plan B. He's a superior piece of emotional real estate. You, however, don't have the emotional forti-tude to fight off his nitpicking criticism. You try, but you exhaust yourself in the process. A therapist may offer point-ers that help the two of you be kinder and more intimate and trusting with each other. This connection is definitely worth pursuing and absolutely worth saving when you hit an emotional bump in the road. Because Gem is so curious about everything from the sublime to calculating the weight of a dust bunny you neglected to pick up, he's quite a conversationalist. There will be times when you finally get tired of the prattle of his voice and just tell him to pipe down. He's not used to people talking to him that way. Just one more reason why he finds you so intriguing.

The Bottom Line: Looking for balance and deeper awareness? This one provides both. You may occasionally run and hide from his nonstop conversation, but overall, this is a winner. **Rating: ****

Sagittarius + Cancer

This borders on obsession. You may barely notice him at first, but once you do, you're gone, baby, gone. You can't get this man out of your mind during the day or out of your fantasies at night. He's so different from you—less bold, far less independent, glued to his family (i.e., his identity), and extremely charming. You can't get enough of this guy. It's like a love addiction that you never want to shake. So you break all your rules and gradually start adapting to his habits, lifestyle, family, and world. You're both extremely sensitive and tend to be loners, so this constitutes a "you and me against the world" bond that is very potent. There are plenty of adjustment problems built into this semisacrificial alliance. You might have to work very hard to make him happy. Is it worth it? *Yes!*

The Bottom Line: This relationship occurs when you're in a state of transition. Your connection with Cancer actually helps accelerate the transition. This one gets big props for emotional and spiritual growth. The heat factor is off the charts, too. **Rating: ****

Sagittarius + Leo

Leo can't get over how bizarre and witty you are. He especially loves your sardonic social commentary. You speak with authority, winning Leo's respect and admiration. Leo makes sure you always look stunning for special events, trips, and romantic evenings. He's very fashion and beauty conscious, so even if you forgot to slip on your Manolos and are still wearing tennis shoes underneath your long evening gown, he wisely brings the perfect pair of shoes along and helps you pull yourself together when the limo arrives. You really adore each other and also have a tightly knit friendship at the base of this arrangement. This is a strong, long-lasting connection that very little can upset or interfere with. Sure, you'll have to periodically pay homage to Leo's ego, but it's really not work—it's part of loving His Royal Highness.

The Bottom Line: Do not let go of Mr. Leo, as a stylist, lover, friend, or husband. Tell others to keep their mitts off of him. He's yours. **Rating: *****

Sagittarius + Virgo

Virgo works hard to beat the odds and keep things from imploding, often to the point of emotional and physical exhaustion. He's so devoted and sacrificial that you often feel lazy and self-centered. You two instantly complete each other, fight off enemies, and defiantly make a real life, thumbing your nose at the odds. Sure, he sometimes drives you dangerously close to insanity with catty sideways criticism—but then he does something thoughtful and caring. As usual, all is forgiven. Old-time astrologers would tell you to forget it. Modern astrologers see this as viable and worthwhile.

The Bottom Line: If you're willing to pause, listen, and relax, you can create a wonderful connection here. It won't be easy. Depending on your desire to make this work, it can fly like an eagle or sink like a stone. **Rating: *****

Sagittarius + Libra

Old-time astrologers had this pegged as an ideal connection. It can be, but it can also fall apart a bit more easily than originally thought. You have a lot in common: beliefs, communication, curiosity, and idealism. But you differ very strongly in two particular areas—sex and social needs. Mr. Libra is at his best in groups, clubs, and social circumstances. You'd just as soon pay your membership dues and only attend a club or social event once a year, and even that feels like a sacrifice. You also have your own private network of friends, loved ones, and priorities—probably elements that Libra doesn't notice, understand, or participate in. Can you see where this is going? After weeks, months, or years of apparent success, the tide could turn against this relationship, largely because you feel trapped and unfulfilled.

Libra's social activities bore you and his sexual desires are annoying. Next!

The Bottom Line: Although you both plan on making the relationship last, you may gradually grow further apart over time. You're the one who generally exits this connection first. **Rating: ****

Sagittarius + Scorpio

You're smitten and befuddled by Scorpio. He seems very powerful, secretive, and slightly unnerving. You want to know more, but almost have to surgically remove information from him. For a while, this feels like black magic. You know it's probably not ideal, but you are willing to temporarily mortgage your soul for your little Scorpio devil. After a while, however, you get tired of the effort. You knock yourself out to please him, but rarely hear a word in return. Once he stops trying to be affectionate and sexual with you, you really get suspicious and figure that he's got someone on the side. You might be right about that. There's always something going on behind the scenes with Scorpio. Note: Do not reveal anything to Mr. Scorpio that could later prove embarrassing. He invented the art of revenge.

The Bottom Line: Are you up for a dash of suffering with your sex and cohabitation? Don't put much time into this one. He makes a much better detective than boyfriend. If you're emotionally fragile (and most of you are, contrary to the image you project), stay away from this. **Rating: ***

Sagittarius + Sagittarius

Sometimes two signs work well together, and sometimes they don't. You both need space, freedom of expression, and me time. When one of you wanders off, disappearing for a couple hours, the other doesn't question it. A mutual understanding that freedom equals inner peace is a very strong bond. Because you both hate to hurt the other's feelings, you sometimes shade the truth. Bad move. That sort of thing can lead to doubt and anger. Be straight-up honest with each other, even if temporary hurt occurs. Get the tough part out of the way up front and look forward to better times in the near future. Here's an idea: Create a home gym. You can practice yoga, lift weights, use the elliptical trainer, whatever. Share your interests. If sweating together isn't your style, then set up a home theater and watch the movies that you enjoy the most, minus the crowd, parking, etc. Do your best to give your Sagittarius plenty of time and space to tell you something, expressing a complex, deeply felt thought that makes him feel vulnerable. Don't pass judgment and you'll strengthen the bond.

The Bottom Line: A surprisingly strong connection. Shut out the rest of the world. Make your home a sanctuary to find peace and privacy in. **Rating: ****

Sagittarius + Capricorn

Capricorn is amused and confused by you. He doesn't quite know what to make of you, especially when you're too late or early or don't return calls and e-mails. He makes the assumption that maybe you have someone else in your life—or something better to do. If you want to make this work (and it can, FYI) you must earn Capricorn's trust, respect, and confidence. That takes a lot of time. If you're willing to put in generous amounts of time and effort, you can develop a connection that could last the rest of your life. If you're too busy or easily distracted (sound familiar?) you might decide to pass on this, but that would be a mistake. You'll learn a lot from Cappie's financial awareness, business experience, and older-than-his-years wisdom. Capricorn can take your raw, unharnessed talent and turn it into a tempting recipe for ongoing success. Don't miss out on this one. Capricorn could change your life.

The Bottom Line: You walk away from Capricorn with your eyes opened up and a sense of worldliness you didn't have before. The longer you remain in the relationship, the more you learn about the way things are—not just the way they should be. **Rating: *****

Sagittarius + Aquarius

You know how to stay out of each other's way. That's important because you both tend to be lost in the clouds from time to time. Maybe it's because you're both psychic and creative. Or maybe it's your style of blocking out stress and tension. This can really work. You can say anything to Aquarius and never face censure. He gets it, probably already knew it, and isn't even remotely shocked or surprised. You share a love of certain gadgets, eccentric movies, and the art of unrehearsed, very intimate discussion. You both function best in a

small, quiet, private space. Because of your work and responsibilities, you may be forced to engage with large crowds and
unfamiliar settings. The moments you and Aquarius share,
however, are meaningful enough to get you through the next
tough time. You may discover your soul mate in Aquarius.
You really understand one another. You also trust each other
implicitly. Both of you often feel like visitors, rather than permanent residents of planet earth, and share a sense of being on
the outside (by choice) and looking in (probably together).

The Bottom Line: Really special and endearing. This
provides love, comfort, peace, and understanding. What
more do you want? With or without sex, this could last
a lifetime. You connect on a soul-to-soul level. Can't beat
that. **Rating: *****

Sagittarius + Pisces

Well, you certainly share some familiar feelings and experiences. And you're there for each other—not regularly or
reliably, but often enough to keep things friendly. The biggest
issue here is the fact that you're both mutable (emotionally
porous and receptive) and you're a Fire sign (Give me liberty
or give me death!) and Pisces is a Water sign (Mommy!).
Another thing: Pisces commits that heinous crime of getting
underfoot. That really turns you off. You don't want to stop
working on an important project because Pisces suddenly
can't find the can opener. Those pointless, "me so needy"
bids for attention gradually wear you down. They also teach
you to never, ever depend on Pisces for anything.

The Bottom Line: Keep looking and move quickly past

Pisces. He's a great guy with all kinds of baggage that you don't have time to unpack and put away for him. **Rating: ***

What Does the Future Hold?

New, innovative projects and passions start being offered to you on a silver platter in 2011. Consider each idea, suggestion, or career offer. Some may sound (and be) too good to be true. Just examine your options.

The year 2012 makes you yearn to be closer to water. You want to look out your office or bedroom window and see tranquil water. You love to listen waves, too. If you're relocating, look for a place by the sea or a lake.

Between late 2009 through most of 2012, you deliberately recalibrate goals, timing, financial pursuits, and certain business or financial alliances.

How to Interact with a Sagittarius

DO:
- Move out of her way. Space and privacy mean more to Sagittarius than to any other sign.
- Come into this relationship with your own goals, friends, money, and strong self-esteem. Don't expect Sagittarius to rescue you. Chances are, she will—and then leave.
- Keep up-to-date. Sagittarius loves to talk about adventure, history, unsolved mysteries, political intrigue, current affairs, and ethics.

- Bring something substantial to the table. Don't become another one of Sagittarius's backbreaking fixer-uppers.
- Be kind, yet honest. Sagittarius needs to know where the lines are drawn and will take things just as far as you'll allow. Make sure your Saggie has a detailed map of what's okay—and what's not.

DON'T:

- Embarrass your Sagittarius in public. Got something potentially hurtful to say? Do it in private—or download it on your therapist.
- Force friends or family on your Sagittarian. It's okay for you to love certain people, but don't expect Sagittarius to feel the same way.
- Smoke or invite smokers to your home. Even if your Sagittarius is a smoker, she needs gentle encouragement to quit.
- Ask your Sagittarius for money. Instead, explain your situation. If you touch her heart, you'll receive a generous gift—maybe several. No manipulation or exaggeration is necessary.
- Try to stop Sagittarius from pursuing a lifelong dream or goal. Instead, encourage it. Be big and loving enough to be happy for your Sagittarius.

Capricorn

♑

You, You, You

As a young child, your relatives referred to you as "five going on fifty." You felt comfortable with adults and enjoyed being helpful. As a young adult, you scurried up the success ladder, despite being beset with personal, health, and financial dramas. No matter how rugged your life's terrain has been, you've learned to accept it as it is, adapt to each change, and expect far more from yourself than you do from others—true to your Earth sign roots. Even so, you keep going, tough mountain goat that you are. After you've married once or twice and raised a family, the second half of your life is the best part, transforming you into a professional and social legend. You keep getting better as you grow older, defying all the dire, boring clichés. You run your first marathon or participate in your first Ironman competition when you're well into your seventies. An investment you made years earlier finally pays off shockingly handsomely, bankrolling your so-called retirement years in a big way. You keep learning, producing, befriending, creating, and celebrating every day of your busy, learn-by-doing life. It's in your complex character to spend the first half of your life earning your way toward good times and success. The second half of your life is a well-deserved good-karma dessert.

People who don't know you have you all figured out: workaholic, lonely, distant, guarded, and, of course, celibate. People lucky enough to really know you (you're very selective about the company you keep) know the truth: You work very hard and have been known to play even harder. You're rarely lonely but don't discuss most details of your private life (uh, that's why they call it a private life).

It's a fatal error to underestimate you. Capricorn has more second acts than any other sign in the zodiac. And Capricorn women, in particular, remain viable, desirable, employable, and competitive long after their peers have retired and given up. You never, ever give up.

Capricorn is one of the signs of sacrifice, wisdom, and karma. You earn each accolade, opportunity, turn of financial luck, and top job. You're uncomfortable when others give you gifts because it makes you feel indebted to them. And being on the receiving end feels uncomfortably like giving up control. Well, actually, it does involve certain elements of surrender. Your preference is to do the giving, to dole out the dollars and opportunities and maintain full control of your destiny—and to a certain extent, the destiny of others, too.

The first ten days of Capricorn belong to true Capricorns.

If you were born then, you're a type A personality who is obsessive about accountability and responsibility, and a tireless worker. The second ten days of Capricorn are ruled by Taurus, making you very acquisitive, sensuous, and somewhat excessive about everything you enjoy and love. If you love chocolate chip cookies (of course you do), you might eat an entire bag of them in one sitting. The third ten days of Capricorn are ruled by Virgo. This gives you plenty of self-discipline and a tendency to be nervous, to have to battle irritable bowel syndrome, and to be intolerant of lazy slobs who don't pull their own weight.

You're also one of the cardinals: Aries, Cancer, Libra, Capricorn—the go-getters of the zodiac that want results and proof of progress right now. You're the kind of results-oriented person who's been known to say, "I'll believe it when I see it."

You have little or no inclination to get even or walk away with a pound of flesh for wrongs another committed. You're too busy to be bothered with revenge. You do, however, enjoy wearing down your competition, outlasting them, and quietly taking over their companies, ex-lovers, and abandoned loyal friends and assistants. Pragmatic to the core, you refuse to neglect excellent talent and value (even when they reside in a competitor's discards) because of something as primitive and tempestuous as revenge. Again, revenge in your view equals loss of control, which just doesn't work for you.

Trust is less personal to you than it is to many other

zodiac signs (such as Scorpio). You view trust as something that is earned and is generally a fragile, impermanent thing—kind of like hope and baby teeth. You understand the value and importance of trust and regularly employ it in business and personal matters because it's the lubricant that greases the wheels of progress. When trust is broken, you're never surprised. You don't blame another for betraying your trust. You blame yourself for expecting too much from another. And then you pick up your hammer and nails and get started on a new project. To say that you're far wiser than your years is a gross understatement.

Stars with your star sign: Katie Couric, Mary J. Blige, Dolly Parton, Kate Moss, Christy Turlington, Dido, Julia Louis-Dreyfus, Annie Lennox, Diane Keaton, Kate Bosworth, and Faye Dunaway.

If You Were an Animal . . .

Your astrological association with the mountain goat perfectly represents you. You understand from early childhood that life is about what you do—and doing takes effort. At the end of the day, you judge your progress by how high you've climbed, how many tasks you've accomplished, how many mouths you've fed, how many comebacks you've made. You scout for the best trail and then invite others to follow in your footsteps. You have grace and balance and are more persistent than anyone you know. For you, a challenge well met builds a life worth living.

Career and Money

You grow up expecting less of others and a lot more of yourself. This tends to isolate you from a lot of people. While you're busy earning your way through school, helping in the family business, or sweeping floors after hours, your pals are partying. They return after fabulous weekends with hair-raising stories. You sit and listen to their close calls, bemused. When they ask what you did, you always say the same thing: "I worked." Although your fun-loving friends don't see this as a portent, it is. You are the hardest-working, most focused, most persistent and ambitious person in your group. Later on in life, when they're bailing each other out for domestic violence and DUIs, they may run into you again—only this time as the sitting judge at their hearing. You're a quiet, subtle conqueror and understand that nothing is guaranteed to last forever.

Life's impermanence brings out the best in you. You expect to work hard and don't view it as a drag. You enjoy the process of accomplishing tasks that most people would find too taxing. Because of your persistence and dedication during the first half of your life, you generally have more money and security to create an enjoyable second half. Your work ethic isn't learned—it's built-in. No matter how many times you try and fail, you keep on trying until you get it right. You earn your successes and others' respect.

Even though few of your peers recognize what an extraordinary person you are (until later in life), you systematically prepare for a successful future by embracing the necessity of hard work. Your friends view your work ethic with both awe and pity. They think it's too bad that you have to work so hard when their dad pays for their cars, trips, clothes, and education. You, Cappie, like the freedom of knowing that you own your future without being indebted to anyone.

Control, responsibility, honor, duty, and tradition all play important roles in your long journey through life. You can't escape the role of leader, headmistress, CEO, chairman of the board, and wise woman. For someone so responsible and aware of the power of image and public relations, you paradoxically blend business and personal affairs and sometimes pay a high price for the experience (scandal, office rumors, "she slept her way to the top" gossip). You understand that challenges are built into your life. You can accept that.

Health

You, Scorpio, and Virgo have something in common: digestive disturbia. We're not talking about minor annoyances here; we're talking about conditions that interfere with plans and may require medical intervention. When you notice persistent indigestion, bloating, pain, or other upsetting symptoms, call the doctor and get a physical. Don't delay getting help for anything connected to your inner food-processing plant. Some of you struggle with food allergies that create misery after most meals. (Some of you are allergic to dairy products, for example, and blow up like a balloon after a double scoop of chocolate chip ice cream. It's just not fair.) There are ways to control most of your discomfort. Be smart and see your doctor.

Aside from digestive issues, you also may have some orthopedic problems with your knees (often associated with humbleness and obedience) and back. Your skin and hair may be dry and dull and require more pampering. Some of you battle unwanted facial or body hair, while others struggle with thinning hair. Make sure you're eating vitamin-rich foods (broccoli, cabbage, asparagus, legumes, fiber-rich grains, and omega-3–rich fish, like salmon) and getting plenty of calcium, vitamin D, magnesium, and selenium.

Friends and Family

You take all promises you make to heart. Your friends may let you off the hook when you have to cancel plans at the last minute (due to cramps, death in the family, car in the shop, etc.), but you can't erase your sense of duty and obligation. If you shirk a duty, party, or other agreed-upon activity with friends and family, you punish yourself by working harder and doing anything possible to make it up to others. They, of course, expect nothing from you. Yes, Capricorn: It can be said that you take life *very* seriously. And you have standards—big, high ones.

You also feel respectful and interested in your older

relatives. Some family members may grow bored dealing with the old folks' arthritis complaints and Grandpa's hearing loss, but not you. You love listening to their stories. A history buff at heart, you view your older friends and family members as living history. You might even record some of the stories about the Great Depression, flu epidemic, or Roaring Twenties excesses that your friends and relatives are still able to remember.

Love

No one can beat you in stoicism. You got your Ph.D. in it. You're able to delay gratification *indefinitely*, like the spurned lover in *Love in the Time of Cholera*. Time has a different meaning for you. You have a long memory, a tradition of waiting your turn at the wheel, and a deep-seated belief that persistence is next to godliness. Most of the time, your persistence and dogged patience pay off. You get the man, the job, the money, and the spoils that others were too twitchy and shortsighted to pursue. You commit wholeheartedly—or avoid a relationship altogether. When you decide to merge your energy, love, and experience with that of another's, your intent is to remain attached *forever*.

Capricorn + Aries

You admire and enjoy Aries at first. You play off of each other's strengths and weaknesses. You, however, tend to play a cautious, parental role while Aries cracks up cars, collects speeding tickets, and gets kicked out of restaurants for being obstreperous. It's painfully obvious that Aries needs a mother, father, and fairy godmother. You try to do it all, figuring that eventually Aries will grow up, just like you did. Honey, you grew up when you were five. Your Aries is *how old*? He shows absolutely no sign of being a grown-up. And let's not forget your formidable sexual needs. Aries' equipment is, well, more diminutive than you'd like and he seems to be a sexual sprinter. You need someone to go the distance with you, again and again. You can buy Aries all the electronic toys he pesters you for, but it won't translate into adult behavior, sexual satisfaction, or an end to his angry outbursts.

The Bottom Line: Can you accept that Aries is a full-grown baby with no plans to grow up? Is this the kind of person you're willing to settle for? This connection makes loneliness sound like a good thing. Once you get over your love affair with being needed, this experiment is over, thank Goddess. **Rating: ***

Capricorn + Taurus

Taurus understands your deep desire for privacy, intimacy, and commitment. Taurus also understands that he'll get kicked out if he indulges in monogamy lapses. What Taurus doesn't realize is that you know a lot more about his behavior, friends, and background than he's told you. You do your research and are rarely surprised. You may allow him one or two assignations and pretend that you don't know. You make it clear that you will not tolerate his tendency to spread his seed far and wide. Under your guidance, he is eager to be domesticated. Your strength, sophistication, and success impress Taurus. He knows that there isn't anyone on this planet who can top you, so he tries very hard to be the man you will love for life. You totally control this hot, steamy stew of sexy seduction.

The Bottom Line: Earthy and endlessly passionate, you and your Minotaur were made for each other. You're both rather possessive and know that this one is for keeps. You're the perfect mate for him and he for you. Don't let him out of your sight. **Rating: *****

Capricorn + Gemini

This blend is better for Gemini than it is for you. The best part of this relationship, as far as you're concerned, is that it provides a continuous challenge—like being locked in a fun house after hours. Things change before you've had a moment to recover from the last incident, leaving you in a frequent state of watchful alertness. (What stunt will Gem pull next? Did he tell me the truth about that out-of-town trip? Do my friends know something I don't know?) This combination feels more like work than play—not that you have anything against work. You expect to work, pay your dues, and eventually own the business you worked your way up the ranks in. This is an emotional connection that may have developed at work or through a work connection. You never seem to be able to relax and enjoy the rewards and well-deserved fun. In fact, you feel necessary in the same way that a lab rat feels essential: The experiment couldn't take place without you. And then you realize that there are scads of women dying for a chance with your Gem. You even suspect that some of them have already crossed the sexual line with him. You never quite feel safe, secure, and unconditionally loved by him.

The Bottom Line: All work and almost no play make you very tired and blue. You deserve better and you know it. Gemini is snoring and sleeping like a contented dog, while you wake up at 3:00 A.M. in a cold sweat, suspecting that you've been had. **Rating: ***

Capricorn + Cancer

Great match for both of you! You offer sensitive, semi-helpless Cancer the ballast and stability he hungers for. You are a living embodiment of what hard work and perseverance can do. In a way, you're an über-Cancer. You're what Cancer *could be*, if only he made a consistent effort. You are the responsible one, kind of a parental figure for Cancer. Most Cancer men need mothering, even those who staunchly deny this need. You also help Cancer enter into a new social group, rich in opportunity and very well connected. You balance each other beautifully. He brings empathy and sweetness to your determination and accountability. You're both very privately sexy and somewhat touch deprived. You revel in each other's body, love, and vulnerability.

The Bottom Line: This is one of those "till death do us part" alliances. You feel as if you've met your soul mate—and you probably have. **Rating: *******

Capricorn + Leo

You know going in that this won't be easy, but you can't resist Leo's highly charged sexual vibe and charm. You feel addicted to him. In fact, you skip other activities for ten minutes of snuggling with him or even just a glance at him across a busy street. You're willing to change your life, pack up and move to the other side of the world, and make sacrifices for him. He knows he's got you under his sweet magical spell and enjoys toying with your emotions and seeing how far you're willing to bend over backward for him. He views romance as a hunt or game of skill. You feel trapped in his love spell but refuse to give him up. Your life will change, probably dramatically, if you pursue Leo. It could get better or worse. It definitely won't stay the same. The element of risk is hardwired into this connection and is part of the spark that draws you together. There is nothing you won't do to please Leo—and he knows it. Against your better judgment and to keep the peace, you may give up control to satisfy his ego needs.

The Bottom Line: Hot, intensely passionate, and with a hint of Romeo and Juliet blended with Lancelot and Guinevere. This may or may not last, but it will be one of the most life-changing, unforgettable connections you ever experience. **Rating: ******

Capricorn + Virgo

Virgo is someone you can admire, respect, adore, and trust. This is a relationship based on mutual interests, needs, and beliefs. It may start as a student-teacher or lawyer-client connection. One of you may be more experienced or older than the other. Over time, you become equals in every category, and lovers that last for decades, maybe forever. Don't rush through this. Let it rise slowly, like delicious home-made bread dough. Nurture it like the precious thing it is. You learn from and inspire each other. Travel becomes a regular part of your life together. You never stop being curious and enjoy finding undiscovered wonders in various manuscripts, cultures, and even legal briefs. The two of you are a power couple, not to be messed with. You're a solid unit.

The Bottom Line: Total keeper. If you let this one go, you need an intervention. **Rating: *******

Capricorn + Libra

You look at Libra with stars in your eyes. Libra is so attractive and desirable that he's flawless. Once you're able to learn more about Libra, you discover his eccentricities and his overweening need for approval, attention, and acceptance. If you're the main breadwinner, Libra will feel ignored and hurt while you're at work, and scout around for someone more understanding. Eventually you might find Libra a bit, well, spoiled. You might also find him moody, especially after he's had too much to drink. You feel creeped out when he flirts or talks about your private sex life in front of others. Suddenly his perfection flakes away like plaster of paris and leaves an unreliable shell of a man. You understand that you're stronger and more competent than he is, and eventually you lose respect for him. That's when he stops being the god you once thought he was. That's also when you kick him out.

The Bottom Line: No matter how patient and understanding you are, Libra never seems to grow into the image you originally had of him. He just shrinks in importance over time. **Rating: ***

Capricorn + Scorpio

This is another endearing, beneficial blend. You start off as pals, sharing thoughts, secrets, inside info. You graduate to letting each other know how much your connection means. Before you know it, you've happily tumbled into bed and made magic, passionate love. It's really difficult to think of a better partnership. You both value loyalty and stability. You never doubt Scorpio's judgment, taste, or choices, and you even enjoy his friends and their amazing stories. You two can become a very successful team that rakes in loads of money and accumulates prime real estate and objets d'art in your spare time. You enjoy your time together, whether you're working, partying, or attending auctions. Your friends know right away that you're both utterly smitten, even when you deny it.

The Bottom Line: This great relationship can withstand the test of time, including financial shifts and changes in health and appearance. Great match. **Rating: *****

Capricorn + Sagittarius

You've got a rebel on your hands with Sagittarius. Don't bother trying to enforce rules or fencing him in. He'll bolt faster than a wild pony. Because he's so bright and funny and shockingly gifted in the sex department, you give him plenty of chances to redeem himself. Here's what you need to know: *He is Peter Pan.* If that's what you're looking for, well, lucky you. If you'd prefer a well-adjusted, accountable adult, move quickly past Sagittarius. He seems to attract trouble, unwanted surprises, unexpected venereal problems, and legal hassles. You don't need the disruption and embarrassment. True, he's talented in the sack and maybe in the recording studio—but his problems tend to overshadow his assets. If you're willing to be his dependable port in the storm and not get much in return for your sacrifices, this bud's for you. Most of you, however, can do a lot better.

The Bottom Line: You cannot depend on him. You don't even feel comfortable leaving him in charge of your dog, no matter how well he gets along with your pup. **Rating: ***

Capricorn + Capricorn

You are so stunned and amazed by Mr. Capricorn. He's oddly familiar and so different at the same time. He seems to possess some of the same secret fetishes you do, only he actually tells you about them! Private secrets you've kept to yourself for years (things that embarrass you) aren't anything to worry about when you're with him. He understands you, and you feel so at home with him. The only person you actually need is him. Your taste and color palette are similar, if not identical. Your noise tolerance is similar and you both enjoy shutting out the world and listening to music, curling up with a book, or surrendering to mad, private, passionate lust. Finally, you have a man who accepts your flaws as natural, desirable, and lovable. You feel so lucky—and so does he. Looking back, you may find you met years ago, but got separated due to moves, different schools, etc., and missed each other. This may be the second time around on the marriage wheel for one or both of you, and yet it feels like the very first time.

The Bottom Line: Some things are meant to be and this is one of them. You respect, love, and care deeply for each other. All you really need is each other. Besides being passionate lovers, you're the best of friends. Hold on tight. **Rating: *****

Capricorn + Aquarius

You're pretty impressed and amazed by Aquarius. His intelligence and iconoclasm interest and annoy you at intervals. His political views may be similar to yours, but more dug in and extreme. He's never met a conspiracy theory that didn't give him a shiver up his pant leg. You don't quite know what to make of him but are wildly entertained by his antics, genius, and odd beliefs. You've often wondered what UFO aficionados were like—and now you're dating one. (Has he told you the story of his alien abduction yet? That's coming. Has he ranted on about the health care system, crystal children, and secret government plots yet? Oh, he will.) This is all amusing and entertaining for a while, but can grow tedious if he turns out to be all big, honking talk and very little action. You look at him and see raw talent and high intelligence and can't understand why he hasn't *done something* with his life. You might never get a straight answer from him. Let's face it: One of you is right-brained and the other is left-brained. One of you is realistic and persistent and the other is flakier than Grandma's piecrust. He could be a contender—but he's not.

The Bottom Line: When you require compassion and love, he's busy researching space travel. Get a French bulldog if you need someone to talk to. **Rating: ***

Capricorn + Pisces

You and Pisces get along so well. You can talk for hours, in bed, on the phone, or over drinks at the corner bistro. You're both people watchers and notice little eccentricities in strangers. You like to size up others and compare notes with Pisces. There's something so satisfying about just being together. Simple things like running to the grocery store, the veterinarian's office, or an art exhibit are more enjoyable when you're together. Pisces notices tiny details and oddities that you don't. You might recognize someone from the local paper. Together, you're like a couple of comedy skit writers collecting material. The conversation never actually stops. You're at home with each other. You can say anything and not worry about reproach. In fact, two of the key elements of this pairing are acceptance and open communication. You fall in love with each other's ideas, dreams, and hopes. You also appreciate each other's sensuality.

The Bottom Line: Don't pass this up. Give it time to develop. The more you learn about Pisces, the more you come to love him, foibles, illusions, and all. **Rating:** *****

What Does the Future Hold?

In 2011, a restless, on-the-move trend starts that lasts until 2019. You may move a lot and find a once satisfying career repressive and dull. You'll want new people, ideas, and experiences—now.

In late fall 2012, you shift your priorities around. Ditch a former sacred-cow priority for something more interesting, practical, fulfilling, and profitable. Give yourself the green light to change your mind, and you could initiate a beneficial relationship or business that exceeds your wildest dreams.

How to Interact with a Capricorn

DO:

- Respect Capricorn's need for privacy, secrecy, and, occasionally, formality.
- Do learn to enjoy the company of older people. Capricorn loves and respects older friends and relatives and hopes you will, too.
- Be frugal. Capricorn is more impressed by the money you save than the money you spend.
- Be independent and responsible. Capricorn has little or no respect for needy, dependent ninnies.
- Learn a little about history, architecture, politics, and current events so you have something to talk about. Capricorn finds most gossip or tabloid talk dull.

DON'T:

- Break rules or throw traditions into the dustbin— unless there's a damn good reason.
- Neglect or manhandle Capricorn's treasured antiques, books, silver, or family heirlooms.
- Babble just to fill the air with noise. Capricorns enjoy silence more than empty-headed blather.

- Brag about a gift Capricorn gave you. Never mention the price tag, either. That embarrasses Capricorn and makes you look crass.
- Misrepresent your intentions. Capricorn has seen it all and can see through you, too.

Aquarius

You, You, You

People don't understand you. They don't get your jokes about the connection between wormholes and extraterrestrial invasions, and you really don't care. In fact, you're proud to be wired differently than basic carbon life forms.

The way to your heart is to thread a white-hot probe into your intensely busy brain. All transmissions start and end there.

Because you were smarter and more imaginative than most kids, you had disembodied "imaginary" friends—only they were probably angelic messengers like Elizabeth I or Lady Jane Grey. So while you carried on chats with ghostly royalty that no one else could see, your parents kept busy and brushed it off as "something she'll grow out of." (FYI: That amazing little boy in *The Sixth Sense* was every inch a hyperintelligent, misunderstood, vulnerable Aquarius kind of kid.)

You never forget the redneck rude dudes that hooted and

hollered and made fun of your glasses, haircut, and geeky style sense (baggy asexual clothing by unknown Japanese designers, or your standby: vintage). You overcome every miserable put-down and become a brilliant entrepreneurial success. You get even in ways that are elegant and useful, far beyond the comprehension of the dim bulbs that dogged you. While others obsess over old slights, you, in your famous absentminded-professor way, defiantly change the world without giving a damn about others' empty-headed opinions.

Other signs are pretty good at dreaming up a hazy, gauzy version of a 3-D illusion or model, but you actually engineer it, perfect it, and then get it functioning (and selling). That's one of the thousands of traits that separate you from the rest of the dull normals. We just don't get you at all—but really, really respect and admire you.

As the eleventh sign, you may always seem to be in your own world, while paradoxically performing wonderful feats that impart hope, healing, and wisdom to others. You can't stop yourself from being a humanitarian.

You're a member of the triad of intellectually superior Air signs: Gemini, Libra, and most of all Aquarius. You're the top of the genius food chain. The catch is that yours is also a fixed sign: Taurus, Leo, Scorpio, and Aquarius are all notorious for being maddeningly stubborn, obsessive, rigid, literally *fixated* on a goal, and, of course, almost upsettingly sexy. You stubbornly cling to your position, even when there's nothing left to prove or argue about. When you're right, you're right. So, in social situations, stop repelling others by perpetually explaining, defending, and building a case that supports a theory that everyone is no longer interested in. If you can stop yourself from doing this, you'll keep friends for life—and won't bore others.

The first ten days of your sign belong to genuine Aquarians. Although you detest stereotypes, if you were born then you fit the iconic Aquarius profile. The next ten days are influenced by Gemini, emphasizing communication, a gift for mimicry and controversy, and an interest in being the first on your block to think, do, or own something avant-garde. The final ten days are influenced by Libra, giving you warmth, a strong desire to make and keep friends, and an interest in law and ethics.

Stars with your star sign: Nancy Oliver, Jennifer Aniston, Paris Hilton, Oprah Winfrey, Mischa Barton, Ellen DeGeneres, Sarah McLachlan, Vanessa Redgrave, Lisa Marie Presley, Ayn Rand, Alice Walker, and Mia Farrow.

If You Were an Animal . . .

You'd be a graceful, free, expressive, and independent dolphin. Your intelligence and curiosity are mysterious and mystical, much like a dolphin's.

Career and Money

It's difficult being responsible, logical, and methodical like nine-to-fivers when your best inspiration generally occurs at 3:00 A.M. or just before you and your friends close down your favorite pub. Your genius doesn't just prance in predictable circles. It happens without warning, which explains why a number of you are what old ladies used to call "late bloomers," meaning that you basically live hand to mouth for quite some time until you sell your first hit song or create an affordable alternative energy source. You're always just five minutes away from creating a miracle that can change lives, including your own. Once you do, everybody sits up and takes notice.

You might be fascinated with robots and the avatars that populate video games. You love the concept of creating unique pseudo life forms, outrageous hybrids with unbelievable proportions and powers. It's not at all unusual to find genius artistic Aquarian geeks working in video game production, special effects, and marketing. Marketing, however, is better left to the other Air signs (Gemini and Libra) because they're more in touch with what the general public relates to.

Earning a living is essentially distasteful to you. You refuse to dumb down to placate some middle manager's ego. You know you're smarter than all the horny, arrogant boys, but also understand there's a trade-off at every twist and turn on the sticky, morally compromising road to success. Sometimes, damn it, you just have to compromise— not necessarily your ethics, but maybe your usual style; you may need to make the best of it by trying to function in an unfamiliar, slightly repellent social or cultural situation.

You don't do anything just for the money. In fact,

you're the one sign that can't and won't be bought. Over time, you set aside the stupid concessions you made on your way to the top to make others less threatened by your brilliance and superiority and start doing things your way. For you, it's always more about the work, what you're able to accomplish despite impossible odds and repeated rejections. The dollars are merely lemon wedges in your iced green tea.

Being unbuyable is so freaking powerful. While you're too damn smart and busy to be one of the girls (the herd mentality is a snorefest), you will be a superstar in your chosen field and an example of the goodness and spiritual connection we all aspire to. We're watching you, imitating you, and trying hard to live up to the high standards you set. And guess what? It's not easy. At all.

You're the canary in the coal mine. You see trends, moods, and where the economy is heading long before others. Trust yourself and your remarkable prescience. You're tough enough to stare down those who can't or won't get it. You get it—way ahead of schedule. Apply it. Work on your brilliant theory, product, service, or passion, with or without the support of others. When it comes to anticipating what the future will bring, you're an incredible savant.

Health

Even humans mostly composed of stardust (you) have to face up to physical challenges. Yours often involve stress, mood issues, depression, and anxiety. You're supernatural in most respects, but you still have to cope with a group of primitive issues.

Let's talk about peripheral circulation. This, along with other cardiovascular issues, may be part of your family heritage—an unwanted genetic relic that you have to cope with. Don't smoke. You might get away with it for years until a life change suddenly occurs (and not the good kind). Your peripheral circulation has a better chance of remaining or becoming healthy by quitting smoking, like, yesterday. This includes *all* smoking materials, Miss Smarty-Pants.

Your ankles may be weak, prone to sprains, breaks, or varicosity. Don't torment your ankles by living in teetering high heels. Although you are the exception in so many things, you can't escape certain health liabilities if you refuse to live a healthy lifestyle.

And it's not just exercising, eating healthy, and all the clichés you've heard a million times, it's also your *consciousness* you need to be aware of—your state of mind when going about your daily activities, and the way you react to others' behavior. Some of you suffer from panic or anxiety attacks that may require medical attention. These problems can be managed, so don't be a typical fixed sign who ignores all the warnings and hints while continuing, obliviously and stubbornly, to trudge straight to the emergency room.

Friends and Family

Communication plays a huge role in the success or failure of your close (friends) and unavoidable (family) connections.

You often speak in a shorthand that might sound cold, remote, or dismissive to an extremely insecure or jealous friend or family member. You see a problem, call it what it is, and send self-pitying "screaming meemies" straight to the pouting patch. You don't try to explain what you meant until the pathetic one is stable enough to talk without sobbing or throwing one of her kitschy collectibles at you.

You don't mince words or try to please everyone. You speak the truth. Unfortunately, this is just too much for some people to handle. Instead of making a rapid-fire delivery of the unvarnished truth, be sure others are willing to listen, undistracted, and receptive before saying what needs to be said. Keep in mind that if you're too brusque, others will tune you out and your message will be lost.

For you, reality is challenging and interesting enough without the embellished, outlandish ego involvement. You'd rather deal with the issue, problem, or vision for a future endeavor than kiss up to manipulative bores. Unfortunately, every family has at least one whining, manipulative victim—a tragedy on wheels. Family members are in awe of how you handle these notorious basket cases and eventually imitate your fine art of detachment.

Friends offer more options. You bring certain people into your life for specific reasons. Sometimes in really wonderful connections, a relationship lasts a lifetime. But not all relationships are meant to be lifelong ones. They are chapters in your life that teach you something, help you through a rough time, or toughen you up so that you'll never get conned again. Friendship without guilt, heavy expectations, and nagging liberates you. Seek out people who lead independent lives, follow passionate interests, and have no designs for dumping emotional garbage on your shoulders.

Love

You're not a communal person who enjoys having others perpetually underfoot, tugging at your sleeves or interfering with your latest theory. You treasure your space.

You're an idealist who seeks an equally intelligent, private, committed-to-causes partner. You understand hard work and fall in love with what someone does and how someone thinks. The packaging is less important to you than the rush you get when discussing controversial theories. You look for someone who doesn't immediately categorize you as a nerd genius.

You admire people who are less concerned with nuts-and-bolts details and more enthralled with the Big Picture. Mentally, you fast-forward into the future, and solve problems that you sense, ones that average folk never imagine.

Find your ideal mate by seeking someone independent in thought, passionate in belief, and willing to share your latest adventure.

Aquarius + Aries

You two are an A-team on so many levels. You don't overcrowd each other's need for space or privacy. You both have unique interests and friends, and you aren't generally found in the needy category. So, yeah: This could become a strong hookup with staying power. Don't expect that Aries will find some of your tech, medical, or legal journals interesting, but do anticipate great vacations together (the shorter, the sweeter) and strong friendship that may develop into something romantic. Whatever this relationship turns out to be, it does have staying power, mainly because you both respect and admire each other and understand each other's need for privacy. That is one fabulous but rare quality.

The Bottom Line: Sometimes a strong, honest, trustworthy friend is preferable to a hot, uneven, maddening attraction. We cannot place this in the hot category, but we can classify it as a lifetime connection. **Rating: *****

Aquarius + Taurus

Since both of you are fixed signs, you both want to win when a difference of opinion erupts. Differences are pretty constant—probably daily—in this combo, but can generate creative energy and lots of luscious body heat. You might hate each other in the morning, but will adore each other again by nightfall. It's a power struggle, but one worth exploring. Depending on your ability to tolerate drama, slamming doors, and the occasional revenge flirtation, this could last for years. So much depends on your attitude. If you're able to detach (yes, you can!) and feel more bemused than apoplectic with Taurus's world-class stubbornness, you are so in. The key here is to find the humor and accept the situations, traits, and attitudes you will never be able to eliminate from Taurus's repertoire, and you might have a winning, never boring connection. Added blessing: You two can make tons of money together.

The Bottom Line: Detachment is your best peacemaker and relationship saver. Use it generously. Some can make this work; some just can't handle it. **Rating: *****

Aquarius + Gemini

You find Gemini to be utterly fantastic, charming, sexy, brilliant, and nearly as smart as you are. The thing that just draws you to Gemini is his ability to challenge your intellect and argue intelligently about any far-fetched geekish thing you can come up with. Sure, you may eventually win the Nobel Prize, outdoing a worthy Gemini partner or colleague, but don't let go of the real prize: that confounding, good-looking, brilliant Gem of a man. He's pretty stuck on you, too, even though he does tend to fuss about your appearance (beware of sudden weight gains). Children almost always come with this pairing, along with broods of animals and an artistic circle of friends. Because both of you have artistic, musical, or design talent, you may eventually collaborate professionally, turning a love match into a pretty phenomenal business deal, too.

The Bottom Line: Once you've had Gemini, you're unlikely to leave him behind. This is the crème de la crème. Take it and run with it. **Rating: *******

Aquarius + Cancer

You've always got a project if you align yourself with Cancer. He's got mommy issues. He depends on you, no matter how busy, frantic, and overstressed you already are. And if you're not there to hold him and tend to his mostly oral needs, you're just a mean, cruel bitch and deserve to be slimed with moody, angry, little-boy nonsense. But here's the rub: Cancer thinks you're just about the sexiest thing ever. He can't completely figure you out and finds you just cool and distant enough to justify all of his self-pity. You're a bit of a nightmare-cum-wet dream for him. And believe it or not, that might be precisely what he wants. But back to you: This doesn't have much to offer except for additional emotional overload from his frequent downwardly spiraling moods. You feel more exhausted after listening to his whining and kvetching than you do after a two-hour Bikram yoga session.

The Bottom Line: Do you really want to hurt you? Isn't there some other challenge you could immerse yourself in? This works out a lot better for Cancer than it does for you. Snap out of it. **Rating:** *

Aquarius + Leo

This can work out quite spectacularly. Sure, there will be moments when the two of you lock horns and refuse to budge an inch. This is just typical fixed-sign drama. If you're able to work on your communication skills, you can become each other's ballast, keeping things balanced. You challenge each other, sometimes persistently and relentlessly. Ultimately, you each learn a lot from the other. The spark that you generate is physical, intellectual, and spiritual—very durable stuff that can keep love and friendship warm for decades. There might be times when you grow weary of Leo's vanity and need for approval. Just keep in mind when you start feeling irritated that the vanity and neediness can be flipped into passionate warmth and creativity. A lot depends on what you choose to notice first.

The Bottom Line: You really help each other survive, thrive, and see the world through fresh, better-informed eyes. This is a winner. **Rating: ****

Aquarius + Virgo

You're strangely hypnotized by Virgo's quirks, worries, sudden dizzy spells, gastrointestinal woes, and guilt, which never, ever seem to just go poof until after a lot of beer or wine. Virgo is beyond the opposite of you. Virgo is like another kind of droid, which is absolutely a mentally orgasmic experience for you. Virgo feels absolutely everything— even though you feel little or nothing (it's that whole detachment thing). You look at Virgo as a tragic, sexy car wreck that occurs right before your curiously intrigued eyes. You don't understand why he's so worried or upset or a neat freak, but you kind of revel in his bitching about the dust bunny mounds around your bed. He views them as a fire hazard of unknown origin. You'll never find a better housekeeper. That alone makes him worth taking seriously. And then there's the sex. As long as you've very recently showered, he's a stallion in the sack.

The Bottom Line: Do you know how difficult it is to find a great housekeeper/cook/sex partner these days? Give this one a trial run. **Rating: ***

Aquarius + Libra

You're both intellectuals with little bit of kink to keep each other guessing and always slightly on edge. For example, you're never absolutely sure he's completely hetero. (For that matter, you're not altogether convinced that you're something as bland and predictable as 100 percent hetero, either.) But before we wander way out there in existential land, does it even matter? The two of you have such a great time together. There may be a period when you experiment with cross-dressing or adding a third partner, mostly for curiosity's sake, or get carried away on a love, gambling, booze, or drug binge. But again, so what? You seem to always enjoy each other, whatever your sexual proclivities and lifestyle choices happen to be. You two are unlikely to settle into a comfy routine. You're both too experimental for that. You're fashion challenged, giving Libra all sorts of ideas, palettes, and tableaux to play with. You actually give Libra a reason to live, baby. How's that for a humanitarian mission?

The Bottom Line: Leave your inhibitions at the

airport and just see where this thing flies—probably in the face of everything your parents hold dear. Give it a try. **Rating: ******

Aquarius + Scorpio

This has generous servings of pros and cons. For starters, Scorpio cannot resist taking control, keeping secrets, and doing his best to keep you line. Joke's on him, though: No one ever really controls you. It's hard enough for *you* to control you—let alone for some outsider to do it. Anyway, Scorpio's fixation with things being done a certain way can be a brilliant advantage for you. You're kind of hopeless at certain routine domestic chores, so imagine your joy when Scorpio volunteers—*no, insists*—on being in charge, twenty-four/seven, responsible for all kinds of stuff that you never, ever even think about. It's kismet! Or at least it can be. A lot depends on your dignity and desire to be independent. Scorpio's obsession with winning, being right, and getting the final smarty-pants word might drive you to property-damage fantasies. Scorpio views you as *a work in progress*—someone he can mold and improve and possibly (if you're extra good) remain with for an extended period of time. Scorpio remains clueless that you might view him as not much of a challenge, but that's about it. Humor him and enjoy him until you're ready for something more.

The Bottom Line: An interesting experiment that generally doesn't work out. Scorpio, oddly, is the last to know. This is neither an essential nor a rewarding experience. Pass. **Rating: ***

Aquarius + Sagittarius

This combo works extremely well and, flaws and all, can be one of your favorite friendships, obsessions, or love affairs ever. So grab on to mischievous, friendly, excessive Sagittarius—the original bad boy who gives love a bad name. He does have trouble turning down easy, available sex, even after he's apparently been sated by you. He never actually feels sated, which is one reason why he pushes every envelope and excess over the edge. You love the excitement and feel a kind of kinship with this brilliant, slightly goofy outsider. He relates to your mind and is very good with your body. He's open to exploring alternative religious or spiritual paths with you, too. And, like you, he's kind of a dipsy-doodle with money. He's willing to give the shirt off his back (or yours) to someone in need. He's funny and finds something hilarious about your dark, weird periods. No one can bring you out of an emotional funk faster than Mr. Sagittarius. If you're an oddball kind of Aquarius and are strictly seeking security, stay away from Sagittarius. Living with him is just one spontaneous experience after the other—and where do the time, money, and jobs go? Who knows? *Who really cares?*

The Bottom Line: This is great fun as long as you don't take it too seriously. Enjoy your buckin' bronco of a boyfriend, but never leave him unattended with your credit cards or stash of cash within grabbing distance. **Rating: ****

Aquarius + Capricorn

You've got more in common than you might suspect. For starters, you're coruled by Capricorn's ruling planet, Saturn. So no matter how zany and off center you seem most of the time, you still have a pretty good awareness of what works and what doesn't. You also have a superb work ethic, like Capricorn. The trust issue, however, could be a factor. You suspect that Capricorn is shading the truth or flat-out lying. Capricorn suspects that you've actually got more money or sexual experience than you're owning up to. So the battle lines are drawn from day one, creating an uneasy but curious attraction. There's just enough unexpected fascination to keep you attentive, and plenty of secrets for you to pry open. You love sleuthing around when you have the time. Capricorn does, too. In fact, the two of you could cross paths while checking up on each other's stories.

The Bottom Line: Not easy, and sometimes creepy, this still can work—especially if you're able to earn each other's trust and respect. Some of you will be able to manage this. Others won't. **Rating: ***

Aquarius + Aquarius

This is probably too much zaniness for either of you to cope with. Seriously, you often get sick and tired of yourself: Now imagine multiplying that frustration by two. On the other hand, this could work out, provided the two of you attend regular therapy sessions together and apart. Because you know so much about each other—the shared odd desire to try to fly between one high-rise rooftop and another—you feel the strain of too much familiarity and, again, that possibility of alien DNA. This might work out better as two project managers trying to race past each other than anything resembling intimacy, droid-style or otherwise.

The Bottom Line: Skip it. Just watch *Alien* for the ten thousandth time instead. **Rating:** *

Aquarius + Pisces

It's all about your questions concerning Pisces' trust-worthiness and Pisces' dependency issues. You're not good at breastfeeding full-grown adults. A little playful pretend game is okay, but hearing the same plaintive wail day in and day out, "Help me," is too boring and high maintenance for words. It doesn't appear that Pisces will ever actually grow up. He is sincere when he's making promises but totally winging it once he's out of your sight. So if being needed is more fun for you than expanding your mind and experiencing the world, you might be taken in by Pisces' extraordinary charm. The longer you're with him and see how he reacts to stress, pain, and challenges, the harder it is for you to respect or trust him. Good call.

The Bottom Line: Unless you're into giving until it hurts, this doesn't make sense. **Rating:** *

What Does the Future Hold?

Your financial circumstances are likely to go through many ups and downs until 2012 or 2013. By then, you'll figure out a brilliant, low-overhead way to earn a living and build a very satisfying life. Until then, stay out of debt whenever possible.

Between the fall of 2012 and late December 2014, you feel as if you're working harder than usual and have more responsibilities and far less leisure time. Others view you as the best in your field and clamor for your expertise. It's difficult to refuse such attractive offers, but you will have to learn to budget your increasingly valuable time.

How to Interact with an Aquarius

DO:

- Remain open-minded, communicative, and a good listener.
- Understand that Aquarius resents being stereotyped based on any flimsy prejudice or cliché. She's heard them all and will walk away.
- Encourage imagination, silence, and wonder "what if" in existential discussions. Put down the grocery list and think a little bigger.
- Keep a light hand on the control panel. Aquarius may listen to you spew out the rules but will cut and run as soon as possible.

- Respect Aquarius's vision of the future. She is probably right about what may come.

DON'T:
- Make fun of Aquarius's sci-fi interests, biogenetic theories, and conspiracy suspicions. Even when they're pretty funny.
- Try to remodel Aquarius's, um, fashion sense. Let it go. Let her be. Don't throw out the two-sizes-too-large corduroy pants or the collection of Michael Crichton books.
- Betray her. That means Keep Secrets—no exceptions.
- Judge her body. It's enough to be healthy. It's too much to expect movie star perfection.

Pisces

You, You, You

You're heart centered and possess a feeling, reactive nature. When others feel down or angry, you sense it right away. Easily hurt and offended when you're feeling moody and unappreciated, you then switch moods (like a great actress) into a playful, anything-goes adventuress so fast that others' heads spin. Drama is a big part of your nature. You dream of being a dancer, actress, or musician in order to live a beautiful, creative life—with applause from fans, of course. Some of you consider modeling, fashion design, architecture, or photography. Your intention is to mate for life, but, being a romantic who bores easily and who can't bear to be ignored, you sometimes struggle with the limitations of monogamy. Notoriously photogenic, you practice smiling, waving, and walking in front of a mirror, and you always have your favorite music to set the mood. Some of you date musicians, artists, or other performers. Being close to art, fame, and celebrity feels just like home to you.

You have trouble comprehending where your problems end and another's begin. As a result, you cannot resist taking in strays—animal, man, or mineral. Anyone or anything that needs tending gets your sympathy and attention. You also have a lot of luck: You're the one who finds a wad of cash on a busy street or a sweet little puppy or kitten that has been abandoned. People adore your loving nature, eccentric, self-deprecating humor, and passionate desire to please. You're a man magnet—no question about it.

Yours is one of the three Water signs of the zodiac: Cancer, Scorpio, and Pisces are the most sensitive and porous of all the signs. You absorb ambient energy—the barrage of sights, sounds, and smells—and because of that, you pick up the emotional haze of others' conflicted feelings. If you're in a loving, positive relationship and live in a pleasant environment, you feel vibrantly alive, balanced, and safe. If you're in a stressful, ultramoody relationship, your emotions and body absorb negativity and show signs of strain. Avoid takers who use or abuse your gentle, forgiving nature. Avoid people with more problems than you have. You need protective, encouraging, unconditional love around you. Ideally, you're blessed by having someone who categorically worships and fiercely protects you. You need a hero who never hesitates to stand up and defend your honor.

Being born in the first ten days of Pisces makes you a full-blooded, easy-to-recognize Pisces—a creative, sensitive, imaginative, and seductive dreamer. Being born in the second ten days adds a touch of Cancer, making you very practical, somewhat moody, very fertile, and interested in family, real estate, security, and antiques. This group of Pisces is very involved with older relatives and friends and may be connected with a family business or local politics. The final ten days of Pisces are strongly influenced by Scorpio. These Pisces understand money and may be financial savants who attract financial good fortune, smart business partners, and very successful, influential friends. Each decanate produces a very unique type of Pisces.

You're also one of the mutables—Gemini, Virgo, Sagittarius, Pisces—and in fact you may be the most mutable of all. Mutable people are emotionally porous, picking up others' feelings and thoughts without even wanting to. This suggests that you need to be vigilant about the people you align yourself with. If you spend too much time with angry, moody, unstable types, it will affect your emotional balance and mood. You're perhaps the most delicate sign when it comes to emotions—and one of the longest-lived. Since you're going to live a long, eventful life, why not live life to the fullest, do good work, and keep learning, growing, and passing on your accumulated wisdom?

You feel much more at home when you're close to water. In fact, listening to gentle waves rhythmically lap the shoreline is so relaxing that you can stop obsessing and surrender to letting go of stress. Water is a healing element for you. Some of you get so relaxed at the beach that you fall asleep and awaken just as the sun is going down, giving you just enough time to prepare for a splendid date. The sound of water also stimulates pleasant healing dreams. Your body's rhythm blends easily with water, bringing you into balance and a state of grace.

Stars with your star sign: Jessica Biel, Eva Mendes, Carrie Underwood, Drew Barrymore, Eva Longoria Parker, Queen Latifah, Juliette Binoche, Holly Hunter, Cindy Crawford, and Chelsea Clinton.

If You Were an Animal . . .

You'd be a butterfly emerging from its chrysalis—free, alighting on flowers, flitting about and impressing others with your beauty and grace.

Career and Money

Your dream is to be a prima ballerina. Short of that, you'd enjoy living like a celebutante or hot actress on the rise, photographed on the red carpet, dripping in diamonds and tanzanite (the stone that brings out your incredible eyes).

If the glamorous life seems out of reach, you feed your need for beauty and escape by obsessing over your favorite art (you'll go through many art phases), movies, books, actors, and escapist TV series that focus mainly on improbable, once-in-a-lifetime love. You identify with the characters and develop a robust talent for imitating famous people.

Okay, so many of you are working in a cubicle in a

medical office or federal building, filing, typing, and working the phones; but you still manage to find a way to leaf through your favorite celeb magazine and pretend that you're living *that life.*

Some career areas to consider outside of arts and entertainment are medicine; hospital, prison, and nursing home management; veterinary medicine; fashion design; architecture; interior design; and hospitality—bars, restaurants, and hotels.

Money is important, but not the most meaningful thing in your life. You want comfort and security; anything more than that is pure luxury. You have a penchant for fine fabrics, such as silk and cashmere, and jewelry, plus you can rock a little black dress with the right strands of silver, platinum, and gems (especially black opals surrounded by diamonds, tanzanite, Paraiba tourmalines, or pearls) and "come and get me now" pumps.

Health

You're one of the longest-lived signs in the zodiac, despite your tendency to overdo your favorite sins: smoking, drinking, pharming, munching, and staying up late because you don't want to miss your favorite tearjerker movie. A lot of you are night owls who tend to sleep in and miss the morning news. You believe that too much reality is depressing and would rather create a romantic, happy world of your own. When you make friends, you stay in touch for years to come, even when great distances and oceans of time keep you apart. Having good friends is essential.

Pisces rules the feet. It just so happens that most Pisces (even marathon-running, iron-pumping, kung fu–fighting jocks) have beautiful, but still sensitive feet. You love shoes of all kinds, but are in awe of sexy sky-high heels that add height, drama, and sophistication. You're willing to skip a couple weeks of lunches in exchange for an enviable pair of Christian Louboutin or Dior shoes. Eventually even the most fashion conscious among you must learn to make peace with lower heels, or even flats. A Pisces with throbbing bunions and fallen arches is an unhappy, moody girl. So while you're making friends with the salespeople at your favorite drop-dead gorgeous shoe store, learn to love your friendly neighborhood podiatrist, too. To keep your muscles lengthened and lithe, engage in regular swimming, walking, dancing, yoga, and Pilates. And no matter what form of exercise you choose, be sure to turn on your favorite music. It makes exercise seem almost enjoyable.

Friends and Family

You love studying your family roots and country of origin. You adore traditions but don't like feeling limited by them. After you make it through your teenage years and are able to express your independence and feel less dominated by your parents' lofty expectations, you learn to love and respect your parents even more. You are a family person who goes out of her way to keep the family together and up-to-date on every new marriage, birth, or illness.

You're a big softy. You're the one who cries at your sister's wedding and sobs each time a new niece or nephew is born. And speaking of babies, you love them. Your biggest hesitation about having your own kids is fear. You don't want to go through labor and have ugly stretch marks, and you certainly don't want anything awful to happen to your kids. Some of you wake up in a cold sweat after having nightmares about this. In true Pisces fashion, you might decide to procrastinate on having children, though you love to spend quality time spoiling your sister's kids rotten.

You love holiday decorations, food, throngs of friends and family, music, and excitement. Holidays transform you into a happy little child who still believes in Santa. No wonder little kids adore you—you speak their language!

Love

Almost every Pisces becomes the subject of family gossip. Because you're a dreamer with fantastic romantic expectations, you sometimes get your heart broken by men who turn out to be bullies instead of romantics. That rough-around-the-edges bad boy might be more con artist than hot lover. You fall for beautiful losers with sad, rehearsed stories. These guys bring out your desire to rescue and rehabilitate. They also appeal to your rebellious side.

Pisces + Aries

There's something gallant and protective about Aries. You love that he seems like a hero, always there to help you. He enjoys rescuing you as much as you enjoy rescuing others. You admire his physical strength and courage. He seems like a real man—someone you can admire and look up to. You savor drama and romance that drips like warm honey out of a full comb, and you can't help but see him as your Superman. Since both of you are idealists (sometimes perfectionists), can you accept each other as you are? Or do you plan on remodeling your Ram into your favorite movie idol? Your Ram seems eager to help—he'll carry your heavy grocery or shopping bags—but afterward he expects some sort of payoff (a chance to touch, kiss, or hold you). You expect an Aries to be a fairy-tale prince willing to die for you but asking nothing in return. If you're willing to view him as a man, instead of some mythic, magical legend, there's hope. If you're expecting something for you but little or nothing for him, it's hopeless.

The Bottom Line: There's a built-in quid pro quo element in this connection that might not sit well with you. You expect this relationship to be about love, but he needs love, too—maybe more than you're ready to give. If you feel marginalized by his anger, his disappointment in you, or his growing list of demands (mostly because he's not getting enough satisfaction), this blend could get pretty depressing. **Rating: ★★**

Pisces + Taurus

You're an irresistible magnet and Taurus is very willing to surrender to your charms. When the two of you get together, it takes an Act of Congress to pry you apart. The two of you generate so much heat that you contribute to global warming. Push your connection into endless love territory. Taurus makes you feel so beautiful. He loves everything about you—even your so-called flaws. He rubs your feet, without tickling them. He listens to you go on and on about something that hurt your feelings—and then he holds you and makes all the bad disappear. There's almost nothing compelling enough to keep you apart. You understand and respect one another. Mostly you adore each other. No matter how sociable either of you is, you don't need anyone else—just each other. Chances are very good that you'd make very loving, hands-on parents, too. You share a love of animals, everything from geckos to gorillas. You also share a love of healing and doing good works for less fortunate people. You might meet at church or at a rally, become inseparable friends, and then fall madly, hopelessly in love.

The Bottom Line: Sexy, spiritual, sensual, and loving, you two *belong together*. One of the most rewarding relationships in the zodiac. Lucky you. **Rating:** *****

Pisces + Gemini

You're utterly fascinated by evanescent Gemini. He seems completely taken with you, totally focused on your every word, one moment—and then, *wham!* gone the next. You're far from bored, but you may feel a little scared and insecure. For example, when you really need a friend and a reliable shoulder to cry on, he might be too busy to bother, or he may just not pick up any messages from you. That's when you start to question if he's monogamous. So many attractive girls seem to know him *very* well, and he's such a flirt. No matter how young they look, he refers to them as "old friends." You're not sure that you can trust him for a few hours, let alone an entire weekend. And sometimes his version of the truth doesn't match up with what others have told you. If you can't totally trust him, you won't allow yourself to fall head over heels for him, either. So he'll complain that you seem selfish or cold and begin to pick away at your flaws. In a relatively short period of time, you figure out that this is not fun, not especially rewarding, and too argumentative for your sensitive taste.

The Bottom Line: Not recommended. You already cope with insecurity and doubt. Gemini just gives you more to worry about. Why put yourself through this? **Rating:** *

Pisces + Cancer

You understand each other, laugh at the same things, help each other through family dramas, and bolster each other's confidence. This relationship may build slowly over time, and last even longer. You begin as two people sharing similar interests (music, politics, movies, horses) and then cautiously get closer over time. You earn each other's trust by delivering on promises made. The big turning point is when Cancer invites you to a family dinner, complete with his parents, grandparents, and siblings. Once you cross that line, you're in. It's essential that you always tell him the full story. Cancer won't tolerate deception or even little white lies. Tell him the whole truth and nothing but. It takes him a long time to let down his guard, but once he does, it's generally for keeps.

The Bottom Line: This is fun, affectionate, family oriented, traditional, and protective. You feel better together than you do apart. **Rating: *****

Pisces + Leo

You're aware of Leo's charms and Lothario reputation, and you're not nearly as taken with him as he is with you. You have the power and control here. Your Leo might be an aggressive lion socially and professionally, but he's a sweet little kitten for you. You don't put up with any of his usual flirtatious ploys. The fact that you laugh at him intrigues Mr. Leo. You brush him off and bring him down a couple notches, which encourages him to view you as a rare treasure that he *must have*. So even if you're not interested, he will persistently look you up, call, or just happen to be at the same pub or club you are. Some might call this stalking, but Leo isn't the stalking type. He's utterly enchanted by your "eat my dust" attitude. For him, it's a first; for you, it's just practice.

The Bottom Line: You're probably too much for him

and he's most likely not enough for you. If you're look-ing for a brief summer romance or spare date on the side, this might work . . . for a while. Leo is an acceptable placeholder until something more exciting comes along. **Rating: ****

Pisces + Virgo

This one stands up well, no matter what kind of chal-lenges and serious issues erupt. You seem to balance each other quite nicely. You understand each other's fears, hab-its, family dramas, and desires. You are very supportive when either one of you is going through a rough patch. Worrywarts by nature, you lecture each other about safety, mostly because you can't bear the thought of something awful happening to the one you love. Creative, insightful, persuasive, and nurturing, the two of you don't really need a houseful of people to call it a party. You enjoy each other's company more than anything money and popularity can buy. You do share an interest in cuisine and wine, and you may blend travel with culinary lessons or teach each other new photography tricks while exploring other cultures. If you're homebodies (and many of you are) you find almost everything you want and need in a well-kept garden. The two of you need a yard where you can raise healing herbs, edible flowers, and bountiful fruit trees.

The Bottom Line: Pretty close to perfect, even by Virgo's stringent standards. This one could easily last a life-time. Don't let him out of your sight. **Rating: *******

Pisces + Libra

At first, Libra seems cerebral, buttoned down, and almost Victorian about certain habits and activities that are second nature to you. But once you cross the all-important intimacy line, you see another side of Libra—a sexy, unpredictable side. You view him as someone with a past, who isn't telling you everything because he's shy. *Psst*—Pisces: You're right about him not telling you everything, but it isn't because he's shy. It might be because he's hiding something (financial shenanigans, a wife, and maybe even a few kids). By the time you discover that he's not who he pretends to be, you're already too smitten to let the mutt go. He's a challenge and probably decent in the sack; but without trust, what do you have?

The Bottom Line: You feel addicted to love with Mr. Libra, but this addiction could break your heart and collapse your credit score. There are so many better matches that offer loads of real love and trust. Skip it. **Rating: ***

Pisces + Scorpio

You and Scorpio fit so nicely together. Your physical and emotional connection is too potent to resist. Once the two of you get together, it's a done deal. Neither of you is likely to find anyone as compelling, passionate, or easy to love. You gravitate toward each other and melt into each other physically and spiritually, which turns your connection into an unforgettable romance. You see Scorpio as your teacher and your superior. Scorpio sees you as the sweetest peach on the tree. Keeping your hands off of each other will take an extra supply of willpower. Both of you (especially you) are willing to give up other things—existing mates, jobs, your 401(k)s—to be together. This is the kind of life-changing bond that legends are made of. Pisces, you are the brilliant, precocious student Héloïse to Scorpio's dedicated, fallible monk Abelard. Those two forbidden lovers made history in twelfth-century Paris. You can do the same thing right here, right now.

The Bottom Line: You were made for each other. Let love rule. Say yes and never look back. **Rating: *****

Pisces + Sagittarius

You seem so different but have similar creative urges and a shared tendency to take pleasure and pain past the limit and to thumb your nose at authority figures. Sounds like a couple of Hells Angels, doesn't it? What attracts the two of you is your shared dislike of being pigeonholed, limited, or controlled. When you two get together, trouble is all but guaranteed. You're not great "joiners." You both like to shoot from the hip, change your mind without commentary or approval from others, and make up the rules as you go along. Chaos is your middle name—at least when you're together. Here's something to keep in mind: Sagittarius may put you up to something you know is wrong, but you're not as feisty and ornery as Sagittarius. You probably won't get away with skipping out of a restaurant without paying your bill. You'll end up in the pokey, while Sagittarius is cruising on his new bike—and forgetting about you with every passing mile. You'll learn a lot of lessons (some of them harsh) because of your connection to Sagittarius—but seriously, wouldn't you rather read about it instead of live it?

The Bottom Line: This combination isn't good for you and may get you into a series of hellish messes. Run away while you still can. **Rating: ***

Pisces + Capricorn

As long as Capricorn isn't too critical about your messy presentation or penchant for losing jewelry, identification, and money, this spicy blend could work very well. Capricorn may seem strict and somewhat repressed at first. Peel off the conservative exterior and find a man you could fall madly in love with. You understand each other's goals, hopes, and dreams. Capricorn had to grow up fast and learn some rather brutal lessons at a young age and has seemed more mature than his peers ever since. You may have had your share of drama and hurt, but you are so gifted at filtering out things you don't want to see or hear that you weren't as affected by life's lessons as Capricorn was. Sometimes Mr. Capricorn holds that against you and makes cutting remarks. If you can tune out Capricorn's stern spartan side and conjure his sexy, loving, "let me please you now" side, *congratulations.* Capricorn is a great bed partner and a staunch protector of you, your career, your friends, and your reputation. No one is allowed to insult you when he's around (except, of course, him). Keep the romance and your shared love of fine things, spiritual values, and a growing interest in genealogy on the front burner. Shove the occasional disagreement toward the back. You know that attitude is destiny. If you adore this man, learn to overlook his infrequent cranky comments. Never forget that he can make your biggest dreams come true.

The Bottom Line: This is excellent, especially if you allow it to grow over time, building strength each step of the way. You have a lot to offer each other. **Rating: ******

Pisces + Aquarius

You have different temperaments, yet you share some of the same political, religious, and ethical views. You appreciate the same type of humor. Aquarius sometimes appears distant, lost in deep thought, but then he can flip the switch and become warm in a nanosecond. Your loving styles are night-and-day different. You spoil a person rotten, are ultra touchy-feely, and have been known to watch your loved one sleep, sometimes holding your breath so you won't disturb him. Mr. Aquarius probably enjoys your humor and your body but gets cranky when you interrupt his thoughts. This turns out to be a better friendship than a long-lived man-woman connection. You can be friends who periodically avoid each other when you're tired of each other's quirks. Marriage or living together could stress this relationship to the breaking point.

The Bottom Line: Friendship is sustainable, but ongoing intimacy is a huge stretch. Keep looking for someone who doesn't make you feel like a science project. **Rating: ****

Pisces + Pisces

Like often attracts like, especially two Water babies like you. You're both so responsive, and you can sense when to say something and when to wait. You're closely keyed into each other's psyche. When you're both struggling with similar problems, get outside help (therapist, clergyperson, doctor) to help regain your perspective. There is nothing sadder than two unhappy Pisces. When you're both up, you can wear out other partygoers and live off of your emotional high for hours. You look gorgeous as a couple. Stylish without being garish, you arrive and everyone takes a look (and several photos). You two present a picture of bliss and classic style that's never forced or tragically trendy. You establish new trends that others can't wait to experiment with. Of course, you're both happier living close to a large body of water, and you adore uninterrupted time together, minus drop-in visits from annoying relatives or neighbors. You enjoy getting massages together, watching dance (and going dancing), and going to concerts—even when you walk away with nearly deaf ears. The energy of a crowd and the passion of the musicians are worth sacrificing some of your hearing for. You understand each other's needs for security, stability, beauty, love, and comfort.

The Bottom Line: If you love yourself, you'll love your Pisces mate even more. Not quite perfection, but awfully damn close. **Rating: ******

What Does the Future Hold?

The year 2010 is a good one, thanks to Saturn's transit. You feel less pressure and manipulation from friends and loved ones. You don't feel as belittled, blamed, or punished by bosses, your spouse, or your parents, siblings, or close friends, who've been rather judgmental during the past few years. Some of you disband a relationship that has run its course. You feel more confident and liberated—and learn smarter ways to earn, grow, and protect your money, savings, and investments.

Because Uranus finally leaves your sign in 2011, you feel less anxious and on guard. Between 2004 and 2011, you changed a lot, largely because your friends and loved ones went through so much. There were times during this Uranus phase when you hesitated to pick up the phone—*what if it's bad news?* Each big shift demanded that you let go of old habits or attitudes and embrace new ones that were very unfamiliar and uncomfortable—at first.

From 2012 on, you may decide to go back to school and study something you've always wanted to do. Some of you take dance class, while others try out for community theater. Highly domesticated Pisces take (or teach) culinary arts. You feel confident enough to live your dreams instead of simply retreating into them.

How to Interact with a Pisces

DO:

- Get accustomed to Pisces' penchant for changing the story, names, or rules as she goes along.
- Have a sense of humor about the Lucy and Ethel mix-ups and pratfalls that Pisces attracts.
- Offer presents for no reason. Pisces love surprise gifts.
- Give your Pisces a gentle, soothing foot massage without her having to ask for it. Use her favorite naturally scented oil, and treat this as foreplay—*because it is.*
- Comment on Pisces' imaginative language arts skills. Many Pisces are artists, writers, actors, or musicians. Pay rapt, respectful attention to her creative efforts.
- Suggest a shoe date, when the two of you will shop for shoes (for her, of course) and then have lunch at her favorite bistro.

DON'T:

- Forget her birthday, a special anniversary, or the eccentricities that make her special and unique.
- Embarrass her in public, no matter how angry you are. She views you as a friend, lover, and knight in shining armor. Don't destroy her dream.

- Make fun of her love of style; her collection of shoes, bags, autographed napkins, or photos; or her shining moment close to a famous person who may no longer be famous.
- Criticize her for being protective and emotional toward animals and all critters, including guppies.
- Refuse to make love to her. If you do, she will question her femininity and worry that you're auditioning a replacement.